INFLUENCE
Living and Sharing a Life of Wisdom

A *Flexible* Inductive Study on Mentoring

BY JAN SILVIOUS AND PAM GILLASPIE

Unless otherwise specified, scriptures are taken from the NEW AMERICAN STANDARD BIBLE®,
© Copyright 1960, 1962, 1963, 1968, 1971, 1972, 1973, 1975, 1977, 1995 by The Lockman Foundation.
Used by permission. (www.Lockman.org)

Scripture quotations marked (ESV) are from The Holy Bible, English Standard Version® (ESV®), copyright © 2001 by Crossway, a publishing ministry of Good News Publishers. Used by permission. All rights reserved.

Women of Faith is a registered trademark of Thomas Nelson, Inc. and is used by permission.

Precept, Precept Ministries International, Precept Ministries International the Inductive Bible Study People, the Plumb Bob design, Precept Upon Precept, In & Out, Sweeter than Chocolate!®, Cookies on the Lower Shelf, Precepts For Life, Precepts From God's Word and Transform Student Ministries are trademarks of Precept Ministries International.

Influence: Living and Sharing a Life of Wisdom

Copyright © 2011 by Jan Silvious and Pam Gillaspie
Published by Precept Ministries International
P.O. Box 182218
Chattanooga, Tennessee 37422
www.precept.org

ISBN 978-1-934884-82-9

All rights reserved. No part of this book may be reproduced or transmitted in any form or by any means, electronic or mechanical, including photocopying, recording, or by any information storage and retrieval system, without permission in writing from the publisher.

Printed in the United States of America

2011

INFLUENCE
An Inductive Study on Mentoring

Dedication

To Kay who has blazed the trail for us.

To Katie, Lauren, Rachel and Bekah who follow in our footsteps.

Acknowledgments

Thanks so much to Rick, Pete and Katherine for your keen input throughout the process of editing and bringing this book to market. Thanks, Dave, for the cover and layout design. Cress, thanks, for your proofreading and style prowess.

To our families . . . Dave, Brad and Katie . . . Charlie, David, Sandi, Lauren, Luke, Jon, Aaron, Heather, Rachel, Bekah, and Ben. There are not enough words to tell you how much you are loved!

INFLUENCE
Living and Sharing a Life of Wisdom

During certain seasons of life, the land between what was and what will be can be treacherous. For the adolescent looking toward teen years, the graduate on the brink of adulthood or the parents of those new adults adjusting to what lies ahead, life in the land of in-between can be as disconcerting as standing on alien soil. The ground of life shifts and changes and takes on a new and sometimes even exciting face with every new sunrise.

There are others in the land of in-between who are not on the cusp of a new land. Rather they are, in a sense, bound for a time by a life-role. What of those who are mired in the in-between? What of those who by their very life-roles find themselves bound to a season yet called to a purpose? There is a time in the life of many students and adults alike when they feel tethered by the neck to the land of the in-between . . . stuck somewhere between where they've come from and where they're going to—aliens who no longer belong where they've been but haven't yet arrived where God is taking them.

For those in the land of in-between, a godly mentor provides invaluable counsel about the path that lies ahead . . . while the worldly mentor can cause monumental damage.

What does the Bible say about mentoring? That will be our question as we spend the next several weeks discovering how to walk with the wise, how to influence and be influenced by others who follow God fully.

Influence: Living and Sharing a Life of Wisdom is a flexible Bible study—designed with options that allow you to go as deep each week as you choose. If you're just starting out and feeling a little overwhelmed, stick with the main text and don't think a second thought about the sidebar assignments. If you're looking for a challenge, then take the sidebar prompts and dig with vigor! As you move along through the study, think of the sidebars and "Digging Deeper" boxes as that 2% of lycra you find in certain jeans . . . the wiggle-room that will help them fit just right.

Life has a way of ebbing and flowing and this study is designed to ebb and flow right along with it!

Enjoy!

Contents

Week One
Wise Friends Lead to Wise Ways
"Hows" and "Whys" of Mentoring . . 3

Week Two
Mentoring in the Moment
The Art of Paying Attention 17

Week Three
Mentoring for the Long Haul
Leverage through Access and Observation 41

Week Four
Mentoring for the Long Haul, Part 2
Walking with Ruth and Naomi 55

Week Five
Mentoring in the Church
A New Testament How-To Guide . . . 65

Week Six
Mentoring Gone Wrong
Learning from Failed Relationships 79

Week Seven
The Mentoring of the Spirit and the Word
Connecting with the Only Perfect Mentor 95

Week Eight
Empowering Your Legacy
Investing in the Lives of Others . . . 109

Resources 122

INFLUENCE
An Inductive Study on Mentoring

How to use this study

Flexible studies meet you where you are and take you as far as you want to go.

1. WEEKLY STUDY: The main text guides you through the complete topic of study for the week.

2. FYI boxes: For Your Information boxes provide bite-sized material to shed additional light on the topic.

> **FYI:**
>
> **Reading Tip: Begin with prayer**
> You may have heard this a million times over and if this is a million and one, so be it. Whenever you read or study God's Word, first pray and ask His Spirit to be your Guide.

3. ONE STEP FURTHER and other sidebar boxes: Sidebar boxes give you the option to push yourself a little further. If you have extra time or are looking for an extra challenge, you can try one, all, or any number in between! These boxes give you the ultimate in flexibility.

> **ONE STEP FURTHER:**
>
> **Word Study: *torah*/law**
> The first of eight Hebrew key words we encounter for God's Word is *torah* translated "law." If you're up for a challenge this week, do a word study to learn what you can about *torah*. Run a concordance search and examine where the word *torah* appears in the Old Testament and see what you can learn about from the contexts.
>
> If you decide to look for the word for "law" in the New Testament, you'll find that the primary Greek word is *nomos*.
>
> Be sure to see what Paul says about the law in Galatians 3 and what Jesus says in Matthew 5.

4. DIGGING DEEPER boxes: If you're looking to go further, Digging Deeper sections will help you sharpen your skills as you continue to mine the truths of Scripture for yourself.

> ### Digging Deeper
>
> **What else does God's Word say about counselors?**
>
> If you can, spend some time this week digging around for what God's Word says about counselors.
>
> Start by considering what you already know about counsel from the Word of God and see if you can show where these truths are in the Bible. Make sure that the Word says what you think it says.

Week One
Wise Friends Lead to Wise Ways

*Whoever walks with the wise becomes wise,
but the companion of fools will suffer harm.*
—Proverbs 13:20 ESV

It's a buzzword in our culture today. The business world mentors, the church mentors, community groups, schools, and organizations of all stripes pour time and resources and energy into mentoring. What is it, though, and more importantly what does God say about it? Perhaps Solomon, the author of the book of Proverbs, gives us the most concise word on the topic, "Whoever walks with the wise becomes wise." Over the next several weeks, we'll look at God's Word, the Bible, to discover for ourselves what God has to say about mentoring as we look at a variety of mentoring relationships throughout the pages of both the Old and New Testaments of the Bible.

We'll see there is no perfect formula. Mentoring relationships look different and serve diverse purposes in the lives of those involved. In fact (we may as well warn you now!) if you're looking for a slick program to roll into your church, match people up, and punch out perfect little Christians, you're looking in the wrong place. Spiritual growth can never be programmed; it is a work of the Spirit. Our part will be to see the examples God has provided us and learn what He has to teach us.

While the mentors we meet along our biblical journey will vary in their giftings and positions, we'll see they all share one important trait: wisdom. So, let's get started on our quest to discover what God has to say about mentoring.

> **FYI:**
>
> **If You're in a Class**
> Complete **Week One** together on your first day of class. This will be a great way to start getting to know one another and will help those who are newer to Bible study get their bearings.

Week One: **Wise Friends Lead to Wise Ways**

CONSIDER the WAY you THINK

What comes to your mind when you hear the word "mentoring"?

Boundaries in Mentoring Relationships

Boundaries are the simple lines you draw in your head that indicate what you will and won't do. A boundary is a safe line of demarcation that allows the mentor and mentee to understand "the rules." Some boundaries to consider are: *How much time will be invested in this arrangement? Are phone calls appropriate? Should meetings be at appointed times or at more casual intersections? Will the investment of time be limited or is it open-ended?* Mentors draw the boundaries but first they have to be established internally. Then they can be incorporated in relationships.

Have you ever been involved in a mentoring relationship? If so, what was your experience like?

What are some potential benefits from having a mentor? Are there specific areas in your life where you'd like input from a mentor? Why?

What apprehensions, if any, does the idea of mentoring stir up within you?

What potential problems arise in mentoring relationships?

Why do you think the world and the Church have such a love affair with the concept of mentoring? In your opinion, do the world and the Church approach mentoring the same way and with the same objectives? Explain.

INFLUENCE
An Inductive Study on Mentoring

Week One: **Wise Friends Lead to Wise Ways**

If you could have any person for a mentor, who would it be and why?

What qualities do you think are necessary in a mentor? Which of these do you see in yourself and those around you?

OBSERVE the TEXT of SCRIPTURE

As we begin our study of this topic, it's important to remember our goal will be finding out what the biblical view, God's view, is on mentoring. Because the word "mentoring" *per se* does not occur in the Bible, we'll look for mentoring concepts, for relationships showing an experienced generation passing truths on to an inexperienced one.

SETTING the SCENE

We know from the greater context that the speaker in this passage is Moses.

READ Deuteronomy 6:1, 5-7 paying attention to how God told Moses to instruct the people to pass on truth about Him. **MARKING** the pronouns *you* and *your* will help you zero in on some of these instructions.

Deuteronomy 6:1, 5-7

1   "Now this is the commandment, the statutes and the judgments which the LORD your God has commanded me to teach you, that you might do them in the land where you are going over to possess it . . ."

5   "You shall love the LORD your God with all your heart and with all your soul and with all
    your might.

6   These words, which I am commanding you today, shall be on your heart.

7   You shall teach them diligently to your sons and shall talk of them when you sit in your house and when you walk by the way and when you lie down and when you rise up."

ONE STEP FURTHER:

Beat us to the punch!
If you were teaching on mentoring without a study guide, what texts would you go to? What questions would you ask of the texts when you got there? Rest assured, we'll take you on a tour of some of the Bible's main mentoring texts, but if you're looking for an extra challenge, if you're looking to be further equipped, make a habit of trying to beat us to the punch. Instead of simply responding to the questions in this book, think beyond it to what questions you'd ask if you were on your own and where you'd find answers. This study will serve you well with the information it leads you to. It will serve you and the Kingdom even better, though, if it spurs you on to think for yourself as one who is faithful and can teach others also.

Record some questions you think need to be answered below along with potential texts to explore.

INFLUENCE
An Inductive Study on Mentoring

Week One: **Wise Friends Lead to Wise Ways**

DISCUSS with your group or PONDER on your own . . .

As we study mentoring, we'll also learn and practice inductive Bible study skills. You'll be able to use these skills whenever you study the Bible. One basic inductive skill is questioning the text. As we seek answers in our study, we'll ask five W and one H questions—Who? What? When? Where? Why? and How? Let's try it out on Deuteronomy 6:1, 5-7.

Who is speaking in these verses and whose message is he bringing?

Who is he speaking to? How do you know this?

What commandment does he give?

Where should it be fulfilled?

How should it be carried out?

Why is Moses giving the instruction?

ONE STEP FURTHER:

Get a Context for Deuteronomy 6:1, 5-7

If you have extra time, read and summarize the rest of Deuteronomy 6. Context—the environment in which something dwells—is critical to understanding the meaning of a text. Although we'll give you the context you need for this study, you're always better off checking context for yourself. It is part of learning to handle texts accurately. Record what you learn about the context from Deuteronomy 6 below.

FYI:

Make Your Own Marks

Please, please, please feel free to mark the text whatever way works best for you. As we go through the main texts, we'll suggest simple markings to help people get started, but if you already have a system of symbols and colors, go with that. The suggested markings in the lesson are designed to make it as easy as possible for anyone to jump in without a full marking system, colored pencils, and the resolve to mark every word in their Bibles. Know what we mean?

INFLUENCE
An Inductive Study on Mentoring

Week One: **Wise Friends Lead to Wise Ways**

When are the people supposed to teach?

What can we learn from this text about who and when to mentor?

If you apply these principles, what specific people will you focus on mentoring? What age group? Why?

What does passing along knowledge of God presuppose? Where can this break down?

How can you live these principles? With your children? With others who are following behind you? Think in specifics. How can you demonstrate biblical principles in your life all day long?

More on Questions
As you ask questions of the text, remember not every verse will answer every question. Some verses answer *Who?* and *What?* while others answer *When?* and *Where?* Ask questions and follow-ups as appropriate and reason through answers you discover. The more you ask, the more you will find.

Why the New American Standard?
While there are a variety of solid Bible translations on the market today, the New American Standard Version provides an extremely accurate word for word translation of Scripture from the original languages making it a perfect match for an Inductive Bible Study. When going deep in God's Word through study, always opt for an excellent word for word translation. Others are the English Standard and New King James versions.

INFLUENCE
An Inductive Study on Mentoring

Week One: **Wise Friends Lead to Wise Ways**

SETTING the SCENE...

When Moses died, God raised up Joshua to lead His people Israel into the Promised Land. You can read Joshua's story in the biblical book of Joshua. The text that follows comes from the last chapter of the book of Joshua.

OBSERVE the TEXT of SCRIPTURE

READ Joshua 24:31 and **UNDERLINE** the time phrase *all the days* whenever it appears.

Joshua 24:31

31 Israel served the LORD all the days of Joshua and all the days of the elders who survived Joshua, and had known all the deeds of the LORD which He had done for Israel.

DISCUSS with your group or PONDER on your own . . .

How long did Israel continue to serve the Lord?

Based on the text, why did they continue to serve during this time?

Jan Silvious On Kay Arthur

Kay Arthur mentored me when I was a new Christian. Neither of us knew that was what was going on. We were just working out our lives, doing what we believed God had set before us. In the process, however, Kay showed me how to "do ministry." I watched her talk to people, ask hard questions, give hugs to those who needed them and speak strong words in due season to those who were stumbling. When I was watching and learning, I had no idea that my life would take the course that it did. Becoming an author, speaker, counselor and now a coach was never on my radar. Yet, I can look back and see that had I never met Kay, had she not welcomed me to walk alongside her, and had I not had my eyes open to observe, I would not be doing what I'm doing now.

One of my favorite sayings is, "What might have been does not exist, so don't even go there!" I am a firm believer in that truth but I think it can't hurt to look back every now and then at "what might NOT have been" if certain people had not played prominent roles in our lives and mentored us, whether we knew it was happening or not.

INFLUENCE
An Inductive Study on Mentoring

Week One: **Wise Friends Lead to Wise Ways**

OBSERVE the TEXT of SCRIPTURE

READ Judges 2:8-12 and **UNDERLINE** every reference to the generation that arose after Joshua,
including pronouns (they, them, etc.).

Judges 2:8-12

8   Then Joshua the son of Nun, the servant of the LORD, died at the age of one hundred and ten.

9   And they buried him in the territory of his inheritance in Timnath-heres, in the hill country of Ephraim, north of Mount Gaash.

10 All that generation also were gathered to their fathers; and there arose another generation after them who did not know the LORD, nor yet the work which He had done for Israel.

11 Then the sons of Israel did evil in the sight of the LORD and served the Baals,

12 and they forsook the LORD, the God of their fathers, who had brought them out of the land of Egypt, and followed other gods from among the gods of the peoples who were around them, and bowed themselves down to them; thus they provoked the LORD to anger.

> **AN APP FOR THAT:**
>
> **When the ball is dropped . . .**
> Something happened between Joshua and his elders and the next generation. The people of Israel followed Joshua and his contemporary elders (some who survived him for a brief time) but that was it. Even though we're looking at a negative outcome, we still have application. One of many questions we can ask is this: *How can we pass on God's Word so we don't end up with a generation that follows us but forsakes God?*

DISCUSS with your group or PONDER on your own . . .

What do we learn about the generation that lived after Joshua and his contemporaries died off?

Look closely at the verbs in verses 11 and 12 and record specifically what Israel did?

From what you have already studied in this lesson, how had they been warned to guard against this?

Week One: **Wise Friends Lead to Wise Ways**

What positive application can you glean for your life from this negative example?

Digging Deeper

What does the Word say about wisdom?

If you can, spend some time this week digging around for what God's Word says about wisdom.

THE BASICS OF A WORD STUDY: Wisdom

Let's work through this one together. Typically when we're looking at a particular verse, we'll word search words from it to find where they and similar words are used elsewhere. This helps us stay true to the original languages. For instance, from Proverbs 13:20, "He who walks with wise men will be wise, but the companion of fools will suffer harm," we'll find out what the Hebrew word for *wise* is and where else it appears in the Old Testament.

Using the online tool Blue Letter Bible (www.blueletterbible.org) we'd do this:

1. **Type in Proverbs 13:20.** You can change the version to the NASB we're working with, although leaving the default KJV will also work since both are tied to Strong's Concordance Numbers.
   Click the "Search" button.

2. When you arrive at the next screen, you will see six lettered boxes to the left of Proverbs 13:20.
   Click the "C" button to take you to the concordance link.

Week One: **Wise Friends Lead to Wise Ways**

3. **Click on the first Strong number** associated with the word *wise*, in this case 2450, links to the original word in Hebrew. In this case, the word *chakam* is an adjective. Clicking this number will bring up another screen that will give you a brief definition of the word and every occurrence in the Old Testament. You can scan the list to see how the word is used elsewhere. Record your observations below.

4. **Repeat the process by clicking on the second Strong number** associated with the word wise, 2449. You'll note that this comes from the same root but functions as a verb. Again, clicking the number will show you the part of speech and list everywhere the word occurs in the Old Testament. Record your observations below.

Since we want to unearth other words translated *wisdom* in the Bible, we can take another approach to bring these to the surface. Remember that we've already looked at the word group *(chakam)* that returns the most results in the Old Testament, so don't get overwhelmed by the results.

Again entering www.blueletterbible.org in your browser, take the following steps:

1. **Type in *wise* as your search item.** Again, since we're using the NASB as our main translation, change the version in the dropdown box to NASB.

2. **Scan the results for different Strong numbers.** The very first verse returned shows *wise* as Strong number 7919. When you click on this it will return every instance of the Hebrew word *sakal*. Record what you learn about *sakal* and move to the next number.

ONE STEP FURTHER:

Word Studies

From time to time in this study, you'll be encouraged to do a word study to find out more about how a particular word is used in its original language. Here are some simple steps to help you get started.

1. Find the original language word. (See **Digging Deeper** for step-by-step instructions.)

2. Run a concordance search to see where else this word is used in the Bible.

3. Note how it's used in several contexts.
   – Verse, chapter, book
   – Other books by the same biblical author
   – Other books of the Bible
   – Other ancient works in biblical days

4. Compare your findings with scholarly works including:
   – *Strong's Exhaustive Concordance*
   – *Theological Word Book of the Old Testament (TWOT)*
   – *Theological Dictionary of the New Testament* (sometimes called *Little Kittel*)
   – Other Greek lexicons
   – Theological dictionaries and Bible dictionaries and encyclopedias

Remember, secondary sources have their place . . . *after* primary sources!

Week One: **Wise Friends Lead to Wise Ways**

3. **Repeat the process making your way through your search.** The next unique number you'll find should be 8458 in Proverbs 1:5. (Remember, we've already looked at 2449 and 2450 which you'll find all over your list!) Again, record your observations below. Remember, you'll be moving from Hebrew to Greek when you hit the New Testament, so the original words will look significantly different.

When you finish examining the words for *wise*, you may want to run through a second time using *wisdom* as your search item.

Take a few minutes to summarize what you've learned about the words *wise* and *wisdom* in the Bible.

SNAPSHOT

"Pam, you need to find a mentor!"

I was probably 22 years old when my friend Karen—who always challenged me in the faith—said, "Pam, you need to find a mentor!" The thought had never crossed my mind, but Karen was the type who knew how to push my buttons. She knew how to spur me on and before I knew it I had taken her advice, talked through some potential women, and found a mentor. Deb, my first official "mentor," helped me discover and start operating in my spiritual gifts. She introduced me to Precept Bible studies and saw to it that I was trained as a Bible Study Leader. Although Deb and I no longer meet regularly, she has become a close friend and remains a wise influence who I'll call in a heartbeat when life throws a curveball.

INFLUENCE
An Inductive Study on Mentoring

Week One: **Wise Friends Lead to Wise Ways**

SETTING the SCENE ...

The context makes it clear that the *fathers* Paul refers to are the Israelites Moses led out of Egypt.

OBSERVE the TEXT of SCRIPTURE

READ I Corinthians 10:1-11 and **UNDERLINE** every reference to *our fathers*. Include pronouns and synonyms (all, some of them, they, etc.)

1 Corinthians 10:1–11

1 For I do not want you to be unaware, brethren, that our fathers were all under the cloud and all passed through the sea;

2 and all were baptized into Moses in the cloud and in the sea;

3 and all ate the same spiritual food;

4 and all drank the same spiritual drink, for they were drinking from a spiritual rock which followed them; and the rock was Christ.

5 Nevertheless, with most of them God was not well-pleased; for they were laid low in the wilderness.

6 Now these things happened as examples for us, so that we would not crave evil things as they also craved.

7 Do not be idolaters, as some of them were; as it is written, "THE PEOPLE SAT DOWN TO EAT AND DRINK, AND STOOD UP TO PLAY."

8 Nor let us act immorally, as some of them did, and twenty-three thousand fell in one day.

9 Nor let us try the Lord, as some of them did, and were destroyed by the serpents.

10 Nor grumble, as some of them did, and were destroyed by the destroyer.

11 Now these things happened to them as an example, and they were written for our instruction, upon whom the ends of the ages have come.

READ through the passage again and **CIRCLE** every occurrence of the words *example* and *instruction*.

DISCUSS with your group or PONDER on your own ...

What do we learn about this generation?

Week One: **Wise Friends Lead to Wise Ways**

According to verse 11, why were these examples recorded?

What specifics can we learn from this text about how not to live?

Take some time to think through the benefits of processing both positive and negative examples as a way to learn the way to walk. As you do, compare what you have seen in the Scriptures we looked at this week.

What is your main take-away application from the Scriptures we have studied this week? How will it change the way you think and act this week?

INFLUENCE
An Inductive Study on Mentoring

Week One: Wise Friends Lead to Wise Ways

@THE END OF THE DAY . . .

Is mentoring a biblical concept? Absolutely! God specifically instructed the people of Israel to teach their children to pass down to the next generation what they knew of God. Unfortunately, they didn't get the job done and we see the terrible results of their disobedience when the next generation grew up rejecting true knowledge of God.

The Bible tells us to pass down what we know and to learn from the examples of others. Paul says examples were recorded so we can learn from them (often bad examples).

In a couple of weeks, we'll look at some long-haul mentoring relationships between Moses and Joshua and then Ruth and Naomi. Next week we're going to consider mentoring relationships that spring up and flourish in critical moments.

Week One: **Wise Friends Lead to Wise Ways**

Mentoring in the Moment

Then Jethro, Moses' father-in-law, came with his sons and his wife to Moses in the wilderness where he was camped, at the mount of God.

Then Moses bade his father-in-law farewell, and he went his way into his own land.
—Exodus 18:5, 27

Mentoring can seem a daunting task if we come at it thinking we're signing on for a lifetime. Sure, we see some lifelong mentoring relationships in the Bible, but we see far more high-leverage mentoring relationships happening in moments, at critical turns. Mentors come into a person's life for a season and then move on. This week we'll look at a few people in the Bible who can be called seasonal mentors, people who mentor on occasions, sometimes even in a moment.

Elijah passed his mantle to Elisha and was taken to heaven. We don't know how many years they spent together, but the time frame was shorter than the one for Moses and Joshua who we'll look at next week. David sought Samuel when he was being chased by Saul, and Jethro counseled his son-in-law Moses when he saw him overwhelmed by the task of judging Israel.

To stay in order we're going to look at our texts today chronologically.

FYI:

Taking *Kairos* Seriously

Greek has two basic words for time: *chronos* and *kairos*. *Chronos* refers to sequence while *kairos* includes significant events (e.g. the "seasons" of farming).

Romans 5:8 is a prime example of *kairos*. "For while we were still helpless, at the right time *(kairos)* Christ died for the ungodly."

Mentoring doesn't always involve long periods of time. Mentoring opportunities can surface in an instant. If we're not paying attention, though, we can miss them.

INFLUENCE
An Inductive Study on Mentoring

JAN SNAPSHOT

Too much to too many...

The foolishness of being too much to too many always leads to a head-on collision with reality. When you think you can become "all things to all people," you have just tried taking on the role of God.

One of my favorite quotes is, "There is a God and you're not Him." When you think you can become the "sustainer" and the "protector," you need to stop and recognize you have tried seating yourself on a Throne that can only be occupied by One.

Week Two: **Mentoring in the Moment**

JETHRO AND MOSES

SETTING the SCENE...

God has delivered the people of Israel from bondage in Egypt through the leadership of Moses. As we pick up the text we find Moses as essentially the sole leader of a mass of people who have known only slavery.

OBSERVE the TEXT of SCRIPTURE

READ Exodus 18 and **CIRCLE** every reference to *Moses*.

Exodus 18

1 Now Jethro, the priest of Midian, Moses' father-in-law, heard of all that God had done for Moses and for Israel His people, how the LORD had brought Israel out of Egypt.

2 Jethro, Moses' father-in-law, took Moses' wife Zipporah, after he had sent her away,

3 and her two sons, of whom one was named Gershom, for Moses said, "I have been a sojourner in a foreign land."

4 The other was named Eliezer, for he said, "The God of my father was my help, and delivered me from the sword of Pharaoh."

5 Then Jethro, Moses' father-in-law, came with his sons and his wife to Moses in the wilderness where he was camped, at the mount of God.

6 He sent word to Moses, "I, your father-in-law Jethro, am coming to you with your wife and her two sons with her."

7 Then Moses went out to meet his father-in-law, and he bowed down and kissed him; and they asked each other of their welfare and went into the tent.

8 Moses told his father-in-law all that the LORD had done to Pharaoh and to the Egyptians for Israel's sake, all the hardship that had befallen them on the journey, and how the LORD had delivered them.

9 Jethro rejoiced over all the goodness which the LORD had done to Israel, in delivering them from the hand of the Egyptians.

10 So Jethro said, "Blessed be the LORD who delivered you from the hand of the Egyptians and from the hand of Pharaoh, and who delivered the people from under the hand of the Egyptians.

11 "Now I know that the LORD is greater than all the gods; indeed, it was proven when they dealt proudly against the people."

12 Then Jethro, Moses' father-in-law, took a burnt offering and sacrifices for God, and Aaron came with all the elders of Israel to eat a meal with Moses' father-in-law before God.

13 It came about the next day that Moses sat to judge the people, and the people stood about Moses from the morning until the evening.

INFLUENCE
An Inductive Study on Mentoring

Week Two: **Mentoring in the Moment**

14 Now when Moses' father-in-law saw all that he was doing for the people, he said, "What is this thing that you are doing for the people? Why do you alone sit as judge and all the people stand about you from morning until evening?"

15 Moses said to his father-in-law, "Because the people come to me to inquire of God.

16 "When they have a dispute, it comes to me, and I judge between a man and his neighbor and make known the statutes of God and His laws."

17 Moses' father-in-law said to him, "The thing that you are doing is not good.

18 "You will surely wear out, both yourself and these people who are with you, for the task is too heavy for you; you cannot do it alone.

19 "Now listen to me: I will give you counsel, and God be with you. You be the people's representative before God, and you bring the disputes to God,

20 then teach them the statutes and the laws, and make known to them the way in which they are to walk and the work they are to do.

21 "Furthermore, you shall select out of all the people able men who fear God, men of truth, those who hate dishonest gain; and you shall place these over them as leaders of thousands, of hundreds, of fifties and of tens.

22 "Let them judge the people at all times; and let it be that every major dispute they will bring to you, but every minor dispute they themselves will judge. So it will be easier for you, and they will bear the burden with you.

23 "If you do this thing and God so commands you, then you will be able to endure, and all these people also will go to their place in peace."

24 So Moses listened to his father-in-law and did all that he had said.

25 Moses chose able men out of all Israel and made them heads over the people, leaders of thousands, of hundreds, of fifties and of tens.

26 They judged the people at all times; the difficult dispute they would bring to Moses, but every minor dispute they themselves would judge.

27 Then Moses bade his father-in-law farewell, and he went his way into his own land.

READ Exodus 18 again and **UNDERLINE** every reference to Moses' *father-in-law*.

READ Exodus 18 one more time and place a **BOX** around the time phrase *from morning until evening* whenever it occurs.

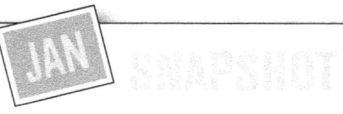

When God Sends the Mentor

I was in a very difficult ministry situation years ago. I didn't know what to do or who to turn to. I'm not even sure I thought God could bail me out because the situation was so sticky. I also knew much of the reason I was in the difficult situation was because of my own blunders, mistakes and wrong thinking. I just didn't have the tools to deal with it and move forward.

I found myself in a radio studio in California interviewing Dr. Marie Chapian, author of *Telling Yourself the Truth*. After the interview, we were having some small talk around the radio desk. I had a very emotional, uncharacteristic reaction to something said. At that point, Marie turned to me and said, "Oh, my Dear, I think God sent me here for you." Little did I know that indeed He had sent her to me. For the next year and a half, she worked with me (by phone and in person) about wrong thinking and how it impacts choices and behaviors.

That event was a cross-roads in my life. Before, I was a "generalist." I could speak about anything, do any kind of Bible study, fit into any kind of event. After, I became a "specialist" in right thinking. Once my eyes were opened, I knew that I never again could speak to women without addressing the fact "how you think determines the course of your life." The encounter took place 3,000 miles from my home. I wasn't looking for help and didn't really think I could get it. I thought it was just up to me but God had another plan and sent the mentor I needed to turn me around.

INFLUENCE
An Inductive Study on Mentoring

Week Two: **Mentoring in the Moment**

DISCUSS with your group or PONDER on your own . . .

What did you learn by marking Moses? What situation was he in?

Common Sense
Bet you dollars to donuts Jethro and Moses never used "mentoring" words. They simply lived a mentoring life. In the midst of established relationships there is no need to pull in mentoring language, *especially* if you are mother- or father-in-law. Simply plan to live by the principles and then live them and let God work.

How much of his time did this consume?

Reuel
In Exodus 2:18 and Numbers 10:29, Jethro is referred to as Reuel, which is thought to mean "friend of God."

What did you learn about Moses' father-in-law?

Carefully consider the interactions between Moses and Jethro. What did Moses do? What did Jethro do?

What did Jethro say to Moses and when? How long did he take and what transpired before he started offering advice?

INFLUENCE
An Inductive Study on Mentoring

Week Two: **Mentoring in the Moment**

What did Moses' father-in-law eventually say about his behavior? How did he suggest Moses deal with the problem?

How did Moses receive this counsel? What did he do?

Do you see any parallels in your life? What situations literally "from morning until evening" wear you down?

How would you or have you responded to wise counsel suggesting you alter your behavior?

As a mentor or wise counsellor, how are you at listening and observing before talking and fixing? Explain. How can you improve in this area?

ONE STEP FURTHER:

Word Study: Father-in-Law

It's important to pay attention to repeated words. In Exodus 18, *father-in-law* is used frequently. If you have some time this week, check out the Hebrew word for father-in-law. Where else is it used in Scripture? Is it a common word? How often does it appear in the text of Exodus 18? Once you have studied the word yourself, consult commentaries and word study helps. Record your observations below.

FYI:

The Priest of Midian

Does the phrase *priest of Midian* strike you as strange? Weren't true priests Levites from Israel's tribe of Levi? At the time Moses sojourned in Midian, the Levitical priesthood hadn't been established, and still Moses' Midianite father-in-law was a priest in a foreign land who appeared to have knowledge of the One true God. It's possible that some Midianites learned to worship the One true God as they were descendants of Abraham through the wife he took after Sarah died.

INFLUENCE
An Inductive Study on Mentoring

Week Two: **Mentoring in the Moment**

Since we're here, let's talk about in-laws. Have you ever considered an in-law a mentor/mentee? How can you apply principles from the Jethro/Moses relationship to your in-law relationship?

I couldn't hear Aunt Gwyn on my own . . .

Several years ago I had a coaching relationship with my husband's Aunt Gwyn. Coaching is similar to mentoring but usually is a time-limited, for-pay situation. In other words, you're asking the coach to give you the truth straight and quick to help propel you forward with the understanding that you'll engage in the process.

Aunt Gwyn, a professional coach who works internationally, did me a big favor coaching me at no cost because we're family. During one of our sessions she had me draw up a chart of my life "roles." I thought I was well within capacity when I faxed her a copy of my chart. The next time we talked, though, the first words out of her mouth were, "Pam, you are way overcommitted!"

Let's just say I didn't receive her assessment well. Oh, I was polite. I did the equivalent of "smile and nod" over the phone, but as Jan would say, "The spirit of 'I'm not having it' simply came over me."

She was telling me essentially what Jethro told Moses . . . you can't keep doing everything you're doing! Moses, though, got it quicker than this girl did!

SAMUEL AND DAVID

SETTING THE SCENE . . .

God has just sent the prophet Samuel to the house of Jesse in Bethlehem to anoint one of his sons as the future king.

OBSERVE the TEXT of SCRIPTURE

READ 1 Samuel 16:10-13. As you do, **CIRCLE** every reference to *Samuel* and **UNDERLINE** every reference to *David*.

1 Samuel 16:10-13

10 *Thus Jesse made seven of his sons pass before Samuel. But Samuel said to Jesse, "The LORD has not chosen these."*

11 *And Samuel said to Jesse, "Are these all the children?" And he said, "There remains yet the youngest, and behold, he is tending the sheep." Then Samuel said to Jesse, "Send and bring him; for we will not sit down until he comes here."*

12 *So he sent and brought him in. Now he was ruddy, with beautiful eyes and a handsome appearance. And the LORD said, "Arise, anoint him; for this is he."*

13 *Then Samuel took the horn of oil and anointed him in the midst of his brothers; and the Spirit of the LORD came mightily upon David from that day forward. And Samuel arose and went to Ramah.*

Week Two: **Mentoring in the Moment**

DISCUSS with your group or PONDER on your own . . .

What did you learn about David from the text? What did you learn about Samuel?

Why was Samuel at the house of Jesse?

Did Samuel know who he was going to anoint? Explain.

What happened to David when he was anointed?

How did the Spirit of the LORD come upon David?

. . . but God helped me hear!

Because God is merciful and persistent, eventually I did "get it." Although I stopped my regular chats with Aunt Gywn, over the course of the next several months, God kept reinforcing the truth she had spoken. The bottom line was I was wrong and she was right. I was over-capacity doing a lot of good things, but not focused on the gifts God had given me.

It took me about a year to pare down and get close to where I needed to be. Aunt Gywn spoke a hard truth that took me a while to swallow, but God used it to change my life. And in case you were wondering, I asked her to forgive me for my terrible attitude even though it was pretty veiled under my "smile and nod."

Starting to say "No" to a lot of good things finally freed me up to have the time to write Bible studies like this. I will always be grateful for her gift of hard truth!

Week Two: **Mentoring in the Moment**

How long did this last?

Start Creating Your Album
Think back to people who entered your life for a season and spoke life-giving truth to you. List them below including what you learned from each.

When Samuel finished anointing David, what did he do?

SETTING THE SCENE...

Saul, the current king of Israel, has attempted to put David to death on more than one occasion.

OBSERVE the TEXT of SCRIPTURE

READ 1 Samuel 19:18 and **CIRCLE** every reference to *Samuel*. **UNDERLINE** every reference to *David*.

1 Samuel 19:18

18 Now David fled and escaped and came to Samuel at Ramah, and told him all that Saul had done to him. And he and Samuel went and stayed in Naioth.

DISCUSS with your group or PONDER on your own...

When Saul pursued David, who did David turn to?

How did David's mentor react? What did he do?

Week Two: **Mentoring in the Moment**

We're not told of any subsequent meetings between David and Samuel before Samuel's death later during the reign of King Saul so we don't know what Samuel might have told David. We do know how David behaved toward Saul and how similar it was to Samuel's behavior toward him. Let's take a look.

SETTING THE SCENE...

Though the Lord commanded Saul through Samuel to utterly destroy the Amalekites, he disobeyed by keeping the best plunder and taking the king alive. Our narrative picks up as Samuel reenters the scene.

OBSERVE the TEXT of SCRIPTURE

READ 1 Samuel 15:26-33. **CIRCLE** every reference to *Samuel* including pronouns and **UNDERLINE** every reference to *Saul*.

1 Samuel 15:26-33

26 But Samuel said to Saul, "I will not return with you; for you have rejected the word of the LORD, and the LORD has rejected you from being king over Israel."

27 As Samuel turned to go, Saul seized the edge of his robe, and it tore.

28 So Samuel said to him, "The LORD has torn the kingdom of Israel from you today and has given it to your neighbor, who is better than you.

29 "Also the Glory of Israel will not lie or change His mind; for He is not a man that He should change His mind."

30 Then he said, "I have sinned; but please honor me now before the elders of my people and before Israel, and go back with me, that I may worship the LORD your God."

31 So Samuel went back following Saul, and Saul worshiped the LORD.

32 Then Samuel said, "Bring me Agag, the king of the Amalekites." And Agag came to him cheerfully. And Agag said, "Surely the bitterness of death is past."

33 But Samuel said, "As your sword has made women childless, so shall your mother be childless among women." And Samuel hewed Agag to pieces before the LORD at Gilgal.

Another Album to Think About

Take some time to think through people you can invest in and how you'll go about it.

INFLUENCE
An Inductive Study on Mentoring

Week Two: **Mentoring in the Moment**

DISCUSS with your group or PONDER on your own . . .

What message did Samuel bring Saul? What had Saul rejected and what were the impending consequences?

What did Samuel do after he delivered the message?

How did Samuel clarify his message? What did He say that the LORD had done?

Just to be absolutely clear, who tore the kingdom from Saul?

What did Samuel do to King Agag of the Amalekites?

Is there any indication Samuel will take physical actions like this one to remove Saul from his kingship? Explain your answer.

ONE STEP FURTHER:

What's the big deal with the Amalekites?

If you have some time this week, run a concordance search on *Amalekite* to learn about Israel's history with this people group. After studying the Word, check secondary resources including Bible dictionaries, commentaries, etc. Record what you find below.

INFLUENCE
An Inductive Study on Mentoring

Week Two: **Mentoring in the Moment**

Digging Deeper

Taking a Closer Look at David

If you have some extra time this week, invest some of it looking at David's character. The question we want to address to the context is *How did David typically react or respond to injustice, foolishness, and godlessness?* As you read, note specific incidents and what happens. In each case do we see David engaging or drawing back, and why? If you want to jump in with both feet, begin in 1 Samuel 16 when David is first anointed and read (or listen) through 2 Kings 5 when his kingship is finally established over all of Judah and Israel. Record what you learn below.

Reference	Injustice/Foolishness/Godlessness	David's Response

Looking at your chart, summarize what you learned about David's patterns of response.

ONE STEP FURTHER:

1 Samuel 15

If you have enough time, read all of 1 Samuel 15 to comprehend for yourself Saul's rebellion and Samuel's subsequent actions. Record your observations below.

Week Two: **Mentoring in the Moment**

FAST FORWARD
SETTING the SCENE...
Having previously halted his pursuit of David to go tangle with the Philistines, Saul resumes his hunt.

OBSERVE the TEXT of SCRIPTURE
READ 1 Samuel 24:1-15. **CIRCLE** every reference to *King Saul* including pronouns, **UNDERLINE** references to *David*.

1 Samuel 24:1-15

1 Now when Saul returned from pursuing the Philistines, he was told, saying, "Behold, David is in the wilderness of Engedi."

2 Then Saul took three thousand chosen men from all Israel and went to seek David and his men in front of the Rocks of the Wild Goats.

3 He came to the sheepfolds on the way, where there was a cave; and Saul went in to relieve himself. Now David and his men were sitting in the inner recesses of the cave.

4 The men of David said to him, "Behold, this is the day of which the LORD said to you, 'Behold; I am about to give your enemy into your hand, and you shall do to him as it seems good to you.'" Then David arose and cut off the edge of Saul's robe secretly.

5 It came about afterward that David's conscience bothered him because he had cut off the edge of Saul's robe.

6 So he said to his men, "Far be it from me because of the LORD that I should do this thing to my lord, the LORD'S anointed, to stretch out my hand against him, since he is the LORD'S anointed."

7 David persuaded his men with these words and did not allow them to rise up against Saul. And Saul arose, left the cave, and went on his way.

8 Now afterward David arose and went out of the cave and called after Saul, saying, "My lord the king!" And when Saul looked behind him, David bowed with his face to the ground and prostrated himself.

9 David said to Saul, "Why do you listen to the words of men, saying, 'Behold, David seeks to harm you'?

10 "Behold, this day your eyes have seen that the LORD had given you today into my hand in the cave, and some said to kill you, but my eye had pity on you; and I said, 'I will not stretch out my hand against my lord, for he is the LORD'S anointed.'

11 "Now, my father, see! Indeed, see the edge of your robe in my hand! For in that I cut off the edge of your robe and did not kill you, know and perceive that there is no evil or rebellion in my hands, and I have not sinned against you, though you are lying in wait for my life to take it.

12 "May the LORD judge between you and me, and may the LORD avenge me on you; but my hand shall not be against you.

TRUE STORIES:

Samuel
To learn Samuel's wider story—how he came to God, what his sons were like, how he followed God, when he died, etc.—read 1 Samuel 1 through 25. Record your summary below.

ONE STEP FURTHER:

The Edge of the Robe
What is significant about David lopping off the edge of Saul's robe or did he just have an overactive conscience when he later felt remorse? If you have time this week, see what you can uncover about the edge of the robe. Start with your concordance and then consult other study helps as needed. Record what you find below.

Week Two: **Mentoring in the Moment**

13 *"As the proverb of the ancients says, 'Out of the wicked comes forth wickedness'; but my hand shall not be against you.*

14 *"After whom has the king of Israel come out? Whom are you pursuing? A dead dog, a single flea?*

15 *"The LORD therefore be judge and decide between you and me; and may He see and plead my cause and deliver me from your hand."*

DISCUSS with your group or PONDER on your own . . .

In addition to the key words you've already marked, what other repeated phrases did you notice? Why are they significant?

What title did David constantly use regarding Saul? Based on the text, why was it important to him?

What opportunity presented itself to David in the cave?

ONE STEP FURTHER:

1 Samuel 24–26
Think about investing some time this week in reading the two full accounts of David sparing foolish Saul's life. The first shows up in 1 Samuel 24, the second in 1 Samuel 26. Sandwiched in between is David's anger toward another fool named Nabal. As you read, record your observations below.

FYI:

David's Heart Struck Him
As much as we praise God for translators who bring Scripture into various languages, the original languages prove so robust that we can miss much of the richness if we decide to avoid them altogether. While the *NASB* tells us that David's "conscience bothered" him after cutting off the edge of Saul's robe, the Hebrew literally says his "heart struck" him. The word play is rich because we expect to see David strike down someone who has been trying to murder him but we see instead *David's heart striking him*. Does it change the meaning of the text? No. Does it add to the richness of the tapestry of the text? Absolutely.

INFLUENCE
An Inductive Study on Mentoring

Week Two: **Mentoring in the Moment**

How did David specifically respond to the urging of his companion to kill the king with regard to:
(1) his own behavior, (2) how he addressed his men, (3) how he spoke to King Saul?

Why didn't he kill Saul when the opportunity was so ripe?

When you are faced with a situation in which you need to respond with restraint, what principles can you take from David here and how will you apply them?

What underlying truth about God held this all together for David? How did David turn his view of God into action?

Can you recount a time in your life when your belief about the character of God (right or wrong) was clearly driving your behavior? Explain.

ONE STEP FURTHER:

Word Study: Anointed

If you have some extra time, take a closer look at the Hebrew word that is translated *anointed*. Ask yourself questions like: *Where else does it appear in the Bible? Who else is it used of? What common New Testament word do you hear in the Hebrew?* Record your answers to these and any other questions *you have* below.

FYI:

From Judges to Kings

Samuel was more than an exemplary prophet of God. His life marked a major transition in the life of the people of Israel. Up until the time of Samuel, Israel was a theocracy. In other words, God was the King. Judges provided human guidance, protection, and deliverance, but God was on the throne. God called Samuel, the last judge, to anoint Saul (and then David) king, thus fulfilling the wishes of the people who wanted a king so they could be like the nations around them.

INFLUENCE
An Inductive Study on Mentoring

Week Two: **Mentoring in the Moment**

How many of David's behavior patterns did his mentor Samuel model? Record as many as you can find.

What practical lessons about restraint have you learned from biblical and contemporary mentors?

SETTING the SCENE...

On the run from King Saul, David and a companion come across Saul's camp asleep. The companion begs David to let him strike Saul dead.

OBSERVE the TEXT of SCRIPTURE

READ 1 Samuel 26:9-11 and **CIRCLE** every reference to *King Saul* including pronouns.

1 Samuel 26:9-11

9   *But David said to Abishai, "Do not destroy him, for who can stretch out his hand against the LORD'S anointed and be without guilt?"*

10 *David also said, "As the LORD lives, surely the LORD will strike him, or his day will come that he dies, or he will go down into battle and perish.*

11 *"The LORD forbid that I should stretch out my hand against the LORD'S anointed; but now please take the spear that is at his head and the jug of water, and let us go."*

Week Two: **Mentoring in the Moment**

DISCUSS with your group or PONDER on your own . . .

How did David refer to Saul in verses 9 and 11?

How does this compare with the plans he knew God had for him?

According to verse 10 what ways did David consider Saul would be taken out?

What was not an option for David in dealing with Saul? Why? How did this compare with the behavior of Samuel?

What application can you make from these examples with regard to waiting on God's timing?

Is there a specific situation in which God is asking you to be patient? How are you dealing with waiting? How can you improve? What specific truths can you call to mind as you wait on God's timing and provision?

Someone to "Believe In"

Other than those I've mentioned, mentors in my life have been short-term but their common trait was they believed in me. It is hard to mentor people you do not "believe in" at their core. Teachers, camp counselors and older friends have been my mentors at one time or another. I don't remember all their names but I do remember that they believed I could become all I wanted to be. That was a critical factor in their effectiveness with me.

Week Two: **Mentoring in the Moment**

Digging Deeper

Waiting, waiting, waiting . . .

This **Digging Deeper** goes out to all of the Type A and recovering Type A personalities. While being a Type A is neither a sin nor an illness, it can predispose people to action and at times make waiting on God more difficult. So this week (especially if you're a Type A!) make some time to see what God says in His Word about waiting on Him. How do we learn to both wait on God and act with Kingdom purposes? Stick with your Bible and record what you learn below.

As you research, consider:

How can I know when God is telling me to wait?

Are there times when I should be acting but I'm paralyzed by fear?

What happens when biblical characters don't wait on God but try to solve problems according to their own time tables? Are there common behavioral clues that we see? How can I learn to see those clues in myself?

What are your symptoms?

There are recognizable (telltale) symptoms of "waiting on God" but not very patiently.

1. Anxiety — always worrying about tomorrow.

2. Overzealousness to be known — *How will anyone know I'm here with this gift and this ministry? What can I do to make something happen?*

3. Jealousy — wanting to guard something from others. *Why did she get that invitation?*

4. Envy — wanting something that another person has. *I should have gotten that opportunity.*

5. Inability to rest — "this moment" is never good enough.

Sounds pretty stressful, doesn't it? Well, it is! God tells us to "cease striving" and for some of us that is a huge, unsustainable demand until we come to the point of relaxing in the fact that "God gives the gift, God gives the ministry and God gives the results." It's in the Book. Look at it in 1 Corinthians 12:4-6.

When you can come to grips with the fact God has given you your gifts, He has given you the place to use them "today" and the effect of that gifting is up to Him, you've won the battle and settled the tension.

INFLUENCE
An Inductive Study on Mentoring

Week Two: **Mentoring in the Moment**

ELIJAH AND ELISHA

SETTING the SCENE...

After an enormous victory over the prophets of the false god Baal and a subsequent depression, Elijah receives some very specific instructions from God.

OBSERVE the TEXT of SCRIPTURE

READ 1 Kings 19:15-16, 19-21. **CIRCLE** every reference to *Elijah* and **UNDERLINE** every reference to *Elisha*. As always include pronouns.

1 Kings 19:15-16, 19-21

15 The LORD said to him, "Go, return on your way to the wilderness of Damascus, and when you have arrived, you shall anoint Hazael king over Aram;

16 and Jehu the son of Nimshi you shall anoint king over Israel; and Elisha the son of Shaphat of Abel-meholah you shall anoint as prophet in your place.

19 So he departed from there and found Elisha the son of Shaphat, while he was plowing with twelve pairs of oxen before him, and he with the twelfth. And Elijah passed over to him and threw his mantle on him.

20 He left the oxen and ran after Elijah and said, "Please let me kiss my father and my mother, then I will follow you." And he said to him, "Go back again, for what have I done to you?"

21 So he returned from following him, and took the pair of oxen and sacrificed them and boiled their flesh with the implements of the oxen, and gave it to the people and they ate. Then he arose and followed Elijah and ministered to him.

DISCUSS with your group or PONDER on your own...

What did God tell Elijah to do in verses 15-16?

TRUE STORIES:

Elijah and Elisha
If you have some extra time, read the rest of their stories @1 Kings 17–2 Kings 13. Record your observations below.

FYI:

Elijah and Elisha
While these two prophets are often mixed up, they are pretty easy to distinguish. Elijah's life and ministry were characterized by big and flashy miracles and events. In one very memorable event Elijah killed 400 prophets of Baal after asking God to send fire down from heaven to consume a sacrifice. At the end of his time on earth instead of dying he was taken to heaven alive in a whirlwind.

God had other plans for Elisha. His life and ministry were important, too; they were just a bit more subtle. He followed God's call during his life and then died like the rest of humanity. Both prophets were important, both fulfilled their roles, but their lives and ministries were different.

INFLUENCE
An Inductive Study on Mentoring

Week Two: **Mentoring in the Moment**

What specific instructions did He give Elisha?

What did Elijah do when he found Elisha? Why? What did it signify?

Stay on the Train

"Pam, God is going to get you where He wants you, guaranteed. You just need to stay on the train." The words sound simple but when Jan spoke them to me during an exceptionally uneventful time in my ministry life, they were balm to my soul. They made me think hard about my striving tendencies and eventually led to a paradigm shift in the way I think and live. Instead of trying to run to where I thought God wanted me, I learned to relax, to be about the business at hand, and trust Him with the results. I concerned myself with obedience and left the "getting there" to Him. Learning to trust Him to drive the train didn't happen overnight, but the more I focused on His sovereignty, the more I learned a new way to live and minister.

Did Elisha understand what Elijah was doing? How do you know?

Who chose Elisha? Explain your answer.

How did Elisha respond?

INFLUENCE
An Inductive Study on Mentoring

Week Two: **Mentoring in the Moment**

What did Elisha do with the oxen? Was this significant? Explain.

Expectations

Mentoring can make for an exciting journey, if it is handled properly. One of the biggest destroyers of good-outcome mentoring is unrealistic expectations. It is important to be aware that if there is anything but a pure heart and sincere desire for spiritual growth and emotional maturity in either party, the mentoring relationship can become a co-dependent arrangement.

Who did Elisha follow?

What did Elisha do for him?

SETTING the SCENE...

We pick up the text as Elijah and Elisha talk prior to Elijah being taken up to heaven.

OBSERVE the TEXT of SCRIPTURE

READ 2 Kings 2:9-11. **CIRCLE** every reference to *Elijah* and **UNDERLINE** every reference to *Elisha*.

2 Kings 2:9-11

9 When they had crossed over, Elijah said to Elisha, "Ask what I shall do for you before I am taken from you." And Elisha said, "Please, let a double portion of your spirit be upon me."

10 He said, "You have asked a hard thing. Nevertheless, *if you see me when I am taken from you, it shall be so for you; but if not, it shall not be so.*"

11 As they were going along and talking, behold, there appeared *a chariot of fire and horses of fire* which separated the two of them. And Elijah went up by a whirlwind to heaven.

Week Two: **Mentoring in the Moment**

DISCUSS with your group or PONDER on your own . . .

What did Elijah ask Elisha in verse 9?

How did Elisha respond? What did he ask for?

What is co-dependency?
Co-dependency happens when you allow the behavior of another person to affect you negatively on an on-going basis. It shows up in the forms of possessiveness, anger, jealousy, control and feeling like you'll die if this person is not in your life. This can turn into "I think I will die, if this person *stays* in my life." For the mentor, it is a skewed belief that the mentee needs her. For the mentee, it is the false assumption that she needs the mentor to be "whole." Co-dependency is a very insidious and all-consuming problem but help is available and sometimes needed to help untangle the people involved.

What can we learn about Elisha based on his request?

How did this narrative end?

Based on the text, did Elijah's ministry end when he was taken to heaven? Explain your answer.

Week Two: **Mentoring in the Moment**

Digging Deeper

Being Who You Are

Perhaps one of the trickiest skills in the mentoring relationship is figuring out how to learn from another person without trying to become a clone of the other person. Think about it. How many kids have grown up wanting to be another Ken Griffrey, Jr. or Peyton Manning? Not to step on any toes here, but how many women have wanted to grow up and be another Kay Arthur or Beth Moore? Being appropriately mentored in the faith will not make you a replica of someone else; it will help grow you fully into the person God intended *you* to be. There's only one Michael Jordan, there's only one Kay Arthur, and there is only one of you. No one else can fill that role!

With this in mind, spend some time this week comparing the lives of Elijah and Elisha. Ask yourself questions like: *What did Elisha learn from Elijah? In what ways were their ministries similar and different?*

In looking at your own life, are you following Jesus in an appropriate fashion? Why or why not?

If not, what needs to change? What thinking and behavior do you need to correct?

If you are mentoring, how do you encourage people to exercise their gifts and flourish in their ministry?

Do you have an "Elisha" in your life you can pass your mantle to?

How will you apply the truths you learned about the relationship between Elijah and Elisha?

@THE END OF THE DAY . . .

Mentors are not always life-long companions. That should be a very freeing thought! As we'll see next week, Joshua served Moses from his youth, observing and learning for years, but some mentors come into our lives only for a season. Some help us to grow up in the faith and then serve as resources and counselors for years to come. Moses didn't meet his father-in-law Jethro until he was over 40 years old and already a man educated by the best Egypt had to offer. Samuel had a profound impact on David when he fled to him in time of crisis, yet from the record we have it appears their time together was relatively short. Mentoring, the pouring of one life into another, can happen over short and long periods of time and can be as different as one person is from another.

Week Two: **Mentoring in the Moment**

Mentoring for the Long Haul

Then Joshua the son of Nun, the attendant of Moses from his youth, said, "Moses, my lord, restrain them."
—Numbers 11:28

One highly significant, long-haul mentoring relationship in the Bible first shows up in the book of Exodus. It is a relationship between two leaders, one named Moses, the other Joshua. God raised up Moses to deliver His people Israel from slavery in Egypt. Although raised in the royal household of Egypt as the son of Pharaoh's daughter, Moses became God's deliverer and led the children of Israel through the wilderness to the border of the Promised Land. It was his successor Joshua, however, who God eventually used to bring His chosen people across the Jordan River and into the Promised Land. The Bible tells us in Numbers 11:28 that Joshua had been "the attendant of Moses from his youth." This week let's see what else we can discover about Moses and Joshua as we turn our focus toward long-term mentoring relationships in the Bible.

> **FYI:**
>
> **Good Spies and Bad Spies**
> Joshua and his friend Caleb were among twelve men sent to spy out the Promised Land. They were the only two who brought back a positive report encouraging Israel to obey God and take the land. Because the other ten spies reported terrifying giants in the land, the people of Israel chose to disobey God. According to Numbers 14:33-34 they were to wander one year in the wilderness for each day the spies had been in the land. Talk about a costly disobedience.

INFLUENCE
An Inductive Study on Mentoring

Week Three: **Mentoring for the Long Haul**

SETTING the SCENE...

Exodus 17 marks the first mention of Joshua in the Bible (although the Numbers account which follows later will refer back to an earlier time in his life). We pick up the story when Joshua on Moses' orders is leading fighting men into battle against the people of Amalek.

OBSERVE the TEXT of SCRIPTURE

READ Exodus 17:8-16 **CIRCLE** every occurrence of *Moses* and **UNDERLINE** every occurrence of *Joshua*. (Be sure to mark appropriate pronouns—my, his, etc.—as well.)

Exodus 17:8-16

8 Then Amalek came and fought against Israel at Rephidim.

9 So Moses said to Joshua, "Choose men for us and go out, fight against Amalek. Tomorrow I will station myself on the top of the hill with the staff of God in my hand."

10 Joshua did as Moses told him, and fought against Amalek; and Moses, Aaron, and Hur went up to the top of the hill.

11 So it came about when Moses held his hand up, that Israel prevailed, and when he let his hand down, Amalek prevailed.

12 But Moses' hands were heavy. Then they took a stone and put it under him, and he sat on it; and Aaron and Hur supported his hands, one on one side and one on the other. Thus his hands were steady until the sun set.

13 So Joshua overwhelmed Amalek and his people with the edge of the sword.

14 Then the LORD said to Moses, "Write this in a book as a memorial and recite it to Joshua, that I will utterly blot out the memory of Amalek from under heaven."

15 Moses built an altar and named it The LORD is My Banner;

16 and he said, "The LORD has sworn; the LORD will have war against Amalek from generation to generation."

DISCUSS with your group or PONDER on your own...

What did you learn about Moses from marking his name in these passages?

FYI:

It's All About God

Exodus 17:8-16 introduces readers to Joshua for the first time in the biblical text and shows him working alongside Moses in a huge victory for Israel. The text also hints at his role as future leader as God commands Moses to write down and tell Joshua that He will "blot out the memory of Amalek from under heaven."

Moses and Joshua filled their roles well but salvation was not from either of them. In days past, God had delivered the people from Egypt through Moses. On this day God defeated the Amalekites while Moses held up a staff and Joshua drew a sword. Regardless of the human leader, the battle belongs to the Lord.

Week Three: **Mentoring for the Long Haul**

We learned in this week's introduction that Joshua had been "an attendant" of Moses from his youth. What further information about Joshua did this text give us?

What specific tasks did Joshua perform? What can we learn from this?

What responsibility for these tasks did Moses give Joshua? How quickly did he have to pull it off?

What did the Lord command Moses to do? Given the situation, why was this significant?

Who was the star of this battle? Whose war was it.? Who will blot out the memory of Amalek?

ONE STEP FURTHER:

The Mountain and the Mayhem

If you have time this week, read Exodus 24 and 32 which recounts Moses and Joshua's journey up the mountain when God calls Moses to meet him and what goes on "back at the ranch" while they're gone. Read the text prayerfully and record your observations below.

INFLUENCE
An Inductive Study on Mentoring

Week Three: **Mentoring for the Long Haul**

SETTING the SCENE...

We saw the trust Moses place in Joshua and how he prepared him for military leadership in the battle against the Amalekites in Exodus 17. In Exodus 33 we see continued trust and further preparation.

OBSERVE the TEXT of SCRIPTURE

READ Exodus 33:7-11. **CIRCLE** every occurrence of the name *Moses* and **UNDERLINE** every occurrence of *Joshua*.

Exodus 33:7-11

7   Now Moses used to take the tent and pitch it outside the camp, a good distance from the camp, and he called it the tent of meeting. And everyone who sought the LORD would go out to the tent of meeting which was outside the camp.

8   And it came about, whenever Moses went out to the tent, that all the people would arise and stand, each at the entrance of his tent, and gaze after Moses until he entered the tent.

9   Whenever Moses entered the tent, the pillar of cloud would descend and stand at the entrance of the tent; and the LORD would speak with Moses.

10 When all the people saw the pillar of cloud standing at the entrance of the tent, all the people would arise and worship, each at the entrance of his tent.

11 Thus the LORD used to speak to Moses face to face, just as a man speaks to his friend. When Moses returned to the camp, his servant Joshua, the son of Nun, a young man, would not depart from the tent.

READ the passage again and place a **BOX** around every reference to the *tent of meeting*.

DISCUSS with your group or PONDER on your own...

What did you learn about Moses from this text?

When Moses entered the tent, what happened?

FYI:

Access
We don't know how much teaching Moses passed to Joshua. The text is silent. What we do know is this—Joshua had the gift of access to Moses' life. Joshua was able to learn by observation and we are wise to do the same whenever we can. Find wise people then watch, listen, and learn.

Give me an hour in the car with that woman...
Back in the winter of 2002 I heard Jan Silvious was going to be the keynote speaker at the retreat our church's conference held annually. I had heard Jan for the first time the previous summer and was struck by her wisdom in applying Scripture to life. I figured someone would have to pick her up from the airport and deliver her to the conference, so I caught Vicki, a woman at my church who I knew was involved in planning the conference, and said, "Hey Vic, if you need anybody to pick up Jan from the airport I'm your girl. I'd love to get that woman in a car for an hour and just learn from her." Later that week Vicki called me to see if I wanted to be Jan's "hostess" for the weekend. Of course I jumped at the opportunity and that's how our relationship first began.

Week Three: **Mentoring for the Long Haul**

How does verse 11 describe the way God spoke to Moses?

What did you learn about the tent of meeting? Was this the tabernacle? Explain.

Why did the people go out to the tent of meeting?

What does the text say about Joshua? How is he described? What was he not willing to do?

What insight does this give you into his character considering verse 7? Compare Joshua's behavior with David's in Psalm 27.

ONE STEP FURTHER:

Where is your access?

Not everyone has access to a Moses, but many of us overlook the access we have to people who can enrich our lives and teach us if we will just slow down and pay attention long enough to listen and observe.

Spend some time prayerfully considering people you want to observe more closely with the intention of learning from them. Record some names below.

Leveraging Your Access

If you have particularly wise people in your life, make every effort to be "around" them. You will learn much from watching them operate, observing how they interact with other people, and looking at the way that they handle difficult situations. Walking alongside is one of the best mentoring positions you can have. Discussion is not always necessary. Focused "time together" is not always important. Being in the same place is a great learning environment. Just remember to look!

INFLUENCE
An Inductive Study on Mentoring

Week Three: **Mentoring for the Long Haul**

SETTING the SCENE...

In response to Moses' cry for help, God has just told Moses to gather 70 men so he will not have to bear the burden of leadership alone.

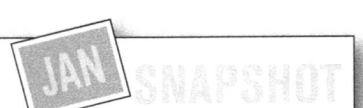

Followers and Leaders...

The younger generation always has to remember that leaders there today won't be there in the future, so they have to pay attention. Understand that you are being nurtured to blossom when the Lord declares the time is right. So, make every effort to be prepared whether you have a personal mentor or not. God has a time and place in history for you to be "His man" or "His woman." That time will come whether the leader you follow now is planning for it or not. Just be wise and let God bring you forth at the right time. It's all His business.

OBSERVE the TEXT of SCRIPTURE

READ Numbers 11:23-29 and **CIRCLE** references to *the Spirit*. **BOX** every reference to *prophecy* (*prophesied, prophets,* etc.)

Numbers 11:23-29

23 The LORD said to Moses, "Is the LORD'S power limited? Now you shall see whether My word will come true for you or not."

24 So Moses went out and told the people the words of the LORD. Also, he gathered seventy men of the elders of the people, and stationed them around the tent.

25 Then the LORD came down in the cloud and spoke to him; and He took of the Spirit who was upon him and placed Him upon the seventy elders. And when the Spirit rested upon them, they prophesied. But they did not do it again.

26 But two men had remained in the camp; the name of one was Eldad and the name of the other Medad. And the Spirit rested upon them (now they were among those who had been registered, but had not gone out to the tent), and they prophesied in the camp.

27 So a young man ran and told Moses and said, "Eldad and Medad are prophesying in the camp."

28 Then Joshua the son of Nun, the attendant of Moses from his youth, said, "Moses, my lord, restrain them."

29 But Moses said to him, "Are you jealous for my sake? Would that all the LORD'S people were prophets, that the LORD would put His Spirit upon them!"

DISCUSS with your group or PONDER on your own...

Who did the LORD place His Spirit upon and what ensued? Were all of the people together?

Week Three: **Mentoring for the Long Haul**

What news did a young man bring from the camp? How did Joshua react?

How did Moses interpret Joshua's concern?

What did Moses say he wished God would do? How was this a correction to Joshua's thinking?

How would you characterize the way Moses corrected Joshua's thinking? What can you learn from it?

SETTING the SCENE...

The setting of the passage is Kadesh Barnea in the Wilderness of Paran. Israel stands poised to enter into the Promised Land. Before they do, however, Moses sends spies into the land.

OBSERVE the TEXT of SCRIPTURE

READ Numbers 13:1-3, 16, **CIRCLE** the words *man/men* as well as synonyms and pronouns and **UNDERLINE** *Joshua*.

Numbers 13:1-3, 16

1   Then the LORD spoke to Moses saying,

2   "Send out for yourself men so that they may spy out the land of Canaan, which I am going to give to the sons of Israel; you shall send a man from each of their fathers' tribes, every one a leader among them."

Where do you invest?
I have a totally different view from many. Instead of mentoring weak people to make them adequate, I focus on mentoring strong people to make them stronger. Weak people may or may not desire to grow strong. Strong people almost always want to be stronger. If that's the case, that strength needs to be leveraged and good mentoring will do that. If there is any mentoring that will help the weak, it will be to help them find their strengths.

ONE STEP FURTHER:

But Moses Called Him Joshua
Numbers 13:16 tells us that Joshua's given name was Hoshea, but Moses called him Joshua. If you have some extra time this week, find out what the names Hoshea and Joshua mean. Then consider what lasting message this had for both Joshua and the people of Israel. Record what you learn below.

INFLUENCE
An Inductive Study on Mentoring

Week Three: **Mentoring for the Long Haul**

3   *So Moses sent them from the wilderness of Paran at the command of the LORD, all of them men who were heads of the sons of Israel.*

16 *These are the names of the men whom Moses sent to spy out the land; but Moses called Hoshea the son of Nun, Joshua.*

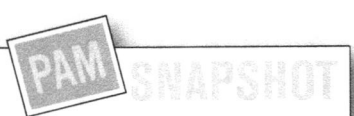

What I Love About Joshua
One of the things I love about Joshua is he never grabbed at power. We don't know exactly when his relationship with Moses began but we do know he served Moses faithfully all of the days Moses lived, bringing Joshua to probably his mid-eighties! That's a lot of years of faithfulness to God and to Moses, especially considering the others who tried to grab power (Korah and his companions) and some of the spotlight (Aaron and Miriam) for themselves. All the while Joshua just stayed faithful.

DISCUSS with your group or PONDER on your own . . .

Based on the text, describe the men sent to spy out the land. According to verse 16, who was among them?

Do you find it surprising that Joshua was a warrior, a leader, and a servant of Moses? Why/why not?

Does this view of Joshua contradict any of your held beliefs about mentoring or being mentored? Why or why not?

SETTING the SCENE . . .

The scene below takes place just prior to Moses' going up to the mountain to die. The people will need a new leader and God says it will be Joshua.

Week Three: **Mentoring for the Long Haul**

OBSERVE the TEXT of SCRIPTURE

READ Numbers 27:15-23. Again, **CIRCLE** references to *Moses* and **UNDERLINE** references to *Joshua*.

Numbers 27:15-23

15 Then Moses spoke to the LORD, saying,

16 "May the LORD, the God of the spirits of all flesh, appoint a man over the congregation,

17 who will go out and come in before them, and who will lead them out and bring them in, so that the congregation of the LORD will not be like sheep which have no shepherd."

18 So the LORD said to Moses, "Take Joshua the son of Nun, a man in whom is the Spirit, and lay your hand on him;

19 and have him stand before Eleazar the priest and before all the congregation, and commission him in their sight.

20 "You shall put some of your authority on him, in order that all the congregation of the sons of Israel may obey him.

21 "Moreover, he shall stand before Eleazar the priest, who shall inquire for him by the judgment of the Urim before the LORD. At his command they shall go out and at his command they shall come in, both he and the sons of Israel with him, even all the congregation."

22 Moses did just as the LORD commanded him; and he took Joshua and set him before Eleazar the priest and before all the congregation.

23 Then he laid his hands on him and commissioned him, just as the LORD had spoken through Moses.

READ the text again and place a **TRIANGLE** over every reference to *the LORD*.

What does commission mean?

The Hebrew word translated *commission* in Numbers 27:19 and 23 is *tsavah*. According to The Enhanced Strong's Lexicon, this word is most commonly translated "command." That said, however, *tsavah* can also mean "to charge" or "commission." Based on the context, we see the idea of commissioning clearly as Moses puts some of his authority on Joshua.

Command implies being *under* authority while commission refers to being *given* authority.

DISCUSS with your group or PONDER on your own . . .

What did God command Moses to do in this passage? Be specific.

According to verse 18, what did Joshua already possess?

Week Three: **Mentoring for the Long Haul**

Based on verse 20, what did God command Moses to put on Joshua? Why was it important for God to tell Moses to do this instead of Moses just picking his own successor?

SETTING the SCENE...

We know from the context that God is speaking to Moses.

OBSERVE the TEXT of SCRIPTURE

READ Deuteronomy 3:28 and **UNDERLINE** all the verbs.

Deuteronomy 3:28

28 *'But charge Joshua and encourage him and strengthen him, for he shall go across at the head of this people, and he will give them as an inheritance the land which you will see.'*

DISCUSS with your group or PONDER on your own...

What did God tell Moses to do to Joshua? What was Joshua going to do?

How well do we model this type of behavior as we bring up leaders today?

Where can we improve as a church? How can we improve in our spheres of influence?

Week Three: **Mentoring for the Long Haul**

Digging Deeper

Character Study on Joshua

If you have extra time this week, you might want to spend some of it investigating the life of Joshua on your own to see what else you can learn about him. Like almost every other major biblical figure, he had both down times as well as up. Here are some tips for your time with Joshua.

Run a concordance search to find out where Joshua appears in the Bible and determine which refer to Moses' protege. Record what you learn from references outside of the book of Joshua.

Read through the book of Joshua asking *Who? What? When? Where? Why?* and *How?* as you go. Record significant observations below.

Based on the text, what were Joshua's greatest moments? Why? How can we learn from them?

What can we learn from Joshua's mistakes? Explain.

> **FYI:**
>
> **It's All About Learning to Follow God**
> Mentors aren't perfect. Moses struck a rock, Elijah ran away from a crazy woman, and Naomi had a whining streak, but they all helped the ones who followed them to follow God in a more complete way.

INFLUENCE
An Inductive Study on Mentoring

Week Three: **Mentoring for the Long Haul**

OBSERVE the TEXT of SCRIPTURE

READ Deuteronomy 31:7-8. **UNDERLINE** the two major commands, one positive and one negative, that Moses gives to Joshua. **MARK** every reference to *God* with a **TRIANGLE**.

Deuteronomy 31:7-8

7   Then Moses called to Joshua and said to him in the sight of all Israel, *"Be strong and courageous, for you shall go with this people into the land which the LORD has sworn to their fathers to give them, and you shall give it to them as an inheritance.*

8   *"The LORD is the one who goes ahead of you; He will be with you. He will not fail you or forsake you. Do not fear or be dismayed."*

DISCUSS with your group or PONDER on your own . . .

Who else was listening as Moses spoke to Joshua? What was significant about this?

What did Moses command Joshua to do? Why, according to the text, should he be able to carry them out?

Is there anything in which you need to be strong and courageous today? If so, what is it?

ONE STEP FURTHER:

To Be . . . And Not To Be
Moses told Joshua the mark to hit and the pit to avoid. If you have some extra time this week, see what you can discover about the following words.

Strong

Courageous

Fear

Dismay

INFLUENCE
An Inductive Study on Mentoring

Week Three: **Mentoring for the Long Haul**

Digging Deeper
Different Kinds of Leaders

How well do leaders pass on what they know? Consider the full context of Scripture as you think through the following questions. This is an open-ended assignment to get you thinking and reasoning on your own, so if you're new to studying the Word, don't panic. Just float on past this one.

For those who are up for the full challenge, consider leaders throughout the pages of the entire Bible. If you want a more focused approach, you may can limit your look to specific leaders, for example the kings of Israel, Judah, or both.

What leaders passed on knowledge and authority both willingly and appropriately? Explain.

What leaders grasped it too tightly to their own demise?

Who gave it up but reluctantly?

What lessons can you learn?

What kind of a leader are you in your realm of influence? How will those who come after you characterize you? Will recalling your life point them to Jesus? Are you a leader who makes followers or other leaders? How much of a distinction is there? How will the results differ?

Be who YOU are!

Learn from others but be who YOU are! This is one of the biggest lessons God has taught me through Jan's influence over the past several years. How often I see people in ministry trying to "be" someone else. We should imitate the faith of those who follow God fully but in a way where we become more fully conformed to the image of Christ, not to the image of another person. Moses influenced Joshua, but Moses was Moses and Joshua was Joshua. Joshua was never supposed to be a second Moses. Paul taught Timothy, but Paul was Paul and Timothy was Timothy.

I have a beat-up old e-mail I carry around in my Bible that ends with these words . . . "Preach, teach, exhort . . . do the work of the ministry . . . Your times of ministry will only become more and more wonderful. You are free to be you in all ways and in all times."

Week Three: **Mentoring for the Long Haul**

@THE END OF THE DAY . . .

Moses and Joshua provide a good example of an Old Testament mentoring relationship. Joshua, a servant of Moses and under his tutelage, was a warrior and leader in his own right. More importantly Joshua was learning to seek God with his whole heart like the man Moses to whom God "spoke face to face as a man speaks to his friend." How does your heart compare to Joshua's today?

Week Four
Mentoring for the Long Haul, Part 2

But Ruth said, "Do not urge me to leave you or turn back from following you; for where you go, I will go, and where you lodge, I will lodge. Your people shall be my people, and your God, my God.
—Ruth 1:16

Last week we looked at a relationship between Joshua and Moses that spanned many years. What began primarily as a master-servant arrangement changed over time as Joshua matured into a warrior and leader in his own right. This week we're going to consider another long-term mentoring relationship but one with a decidedly different twist. Ruth and Naomi offer us a look at a mentoring relationship with "difficult" written all over it. If the fact that they were in-laws wasn't difficult enough, the women also differed in age, came from different countries of origin, and both endured personal devastation and potentially crippling financial loss.

INFLUENCE
An Inductive Study on Mentoring

Week Four: **Mentoring for the Long Haul, Part 2**

OBSERVE the TEXT of SCRIPTURE

Because the book of Ruth is only four chapters, we're going to look at the entire story chapter by chapter. This time you'll want to use your own copy of the Bible. Remember, the setting is during the time of the Judges of Israel, after Joshua but before the Kings.

READ Ruth 1.

DISCUSS with your group or PONDER on your own . . .

Who are the main characters? What were their nationalities and how were they related?

Does anything give you pause about the situation they're in? If so, what?

What tragedies struck the family?

Why did Naomi decide to return to Israel?

When Naomi decided to go back to Israel, how did her daughters-in-law respond?

20s, 30s, 40s, 50s, 60s, 70s

There is no comparison between those years. In the 20s and 30s, you are just finding out who you are in relationship to other people and God. At 40, you begin to settle in and have a clue what life is about. At 50, 60 and 70, you have gleaned great treasures of wisdom that come only from experience. Experience comes with time.

INFLUENCE
An Inductive Study on Mentoring

Week Four: **Mentoring for the Long Haul, Part 2**

What did Naomi tell her daughters-in-law to do? What eventually happened?

What declaration of faith in the God of Israel did Ruth make in this chapter?

Why did Naomi stop fighting her?

What did Naomi say she should be called? Why?

When did they return?

Based on Ruth 1, describe Ruth. What kind of woman was she? Do you think she'd be easy to mentor? Why/why not?

What about Naomi? Would you choose her for a mentor? Why/why not?

Ruths and Naomis Today

The relationship between mother-in-law and daughter-in-law is unique. It has to be carefully cultivated and nourished for it to be healthy and meaningful. The addition of mentoring may or may not work for you. It depends on the relationship.

Don't make any assumptions. Always ask your daughter-in-law what she wants and then respect her choices. (I'm assuming that no mother-in-law would find mentoring a daughter-in-law as anything but pure joy—but that's just my assumption!) So walk respectfully and only give what is desired. There is nothing worse than forced or obligatory mentoring. May it never be!

Week Four: **Mentoring for the Long Haul, Part 2**

READ Ruth 2.

DISCUSS with your group or PONDER on your own . . .

Who was Boaz and why was he significant?

Who took the initiative in this chapter? What additional light does this shed on this character?

How did Ruth and Naomi interact? Were they operating together or independently?

How did Ruth end up in the Boaz's field? Is this significant? Why/why not?

What did Boaz know about Ruth?

How did he treat her? What did he ask her to do?

Living in an Extended Family

Mother-in-law/daughter-in-law isn't the only mentoring relationship that we can grow in our extended families. I'm an only child married to the baby of a family of four kids. In my life this means all my nieces and nephews were born long before my husband and I had children. We were always the cool aunt and uncle who had the sports car and the newest video game systems, but because of our stage in life we didn't spend much time with them as little children. By the time we had kids, the cousins were bigger. We missed something by being . . . late.

Now, though, I've found that I have significant relationships with my adult nieces and nephews because I'm closer in age than the rest of the adult gang.

Week Four: **Mentoring for the Long Haul, Part 2**

How did Boaz tell his workers to treat her?

How did Naomi's outlook begin shifting in chapter 2? Explain.

READ Ruth 3.

DISCUSS with your group or PONDER on your own . . .

What did Naomi set out to accomplish in chapter 3?

What did Naomi tell Ruth to do?

How did Ruth respond?

Would Ruth have known how to navigate the cultural waters apart from Naomi's input? Explain.

ONE STEP FURTHER:

Where do you fit?
If you have some extra time this week, consider how you can specifically be part of growth in your extended family. Who can you learn from? Who can you pour your life into?

INFLUENCE
An Inductive Study on Mentoring

Week Four: **Mentoring for the Long Haul, Part 2**

How do you respond when faced with advice?

Compare Ruth's response here to her response when Naomi wanted her to stay in Moab (in Ruth 1). What is similar and different?

How did Boaz respond to Naomi's plan that Ruth carries out?

How did Boaz refer to Ruth in verse 11? What actions in her life may have led people to conclude this about her?

When people look at your life are they moved to say you are a person of excellence?

What marks excellence today? Why? Is it different for a man and a woman? Explain.

Specific Words for Specific Situations

Doesn't matter how wise of a girl Ruth was; she needed Naomi's help to know how to navigate the local cultural issues involved in asking Boaz to serve as a kinsman redeemer for their family. So often that's the case with us, too. Let's face it, you don't know what you don't know and unless someone who knows helps you out, you're going to be learning some very costly lessons along life's way. It's not that you can't learn on your own; most assuredly you can but it will usually cost you a lot in time, money, and often heartache before you're done.

I love the fact that God sent Jan along my path right after my first book was published to help me with all the stuff I didn't know about speaking, writing, and working with publishers. Her influence and experience has saved me from crashing and burning in a wide variety of ways because she knows the road.

INFLUENCE
An Inductive Study on Mentoring

Week Four: **Mentoring for the Long Haul, Part 2**

What was the one potential glitch in Naomi's plan?

How quickly did Boaz do the right thing?

READ Ruth 4.

DISCUSS with your group or PONDER on your own . . .

How did the closer relative respond to the offer of the land and Ruth?

What did Boaz do?

Who was the child born to Ruth and Boaz?

Who was Ruth's other mother-in-law?

How does mileage affect mentoring?

The wiser you are, the more you realize you often don't have cut-and-dried answers. There is a certain point where it comes to you that other people in the world know a lot more and you don't have a corner on knowledge and wisdom, so you learn to let many things work themselves out. You don't have to have an answer for everything.

INFLUENCE
An Inductive Study on Mentoring

Week Four: **Mentoring for the Long Haul, Part 2**

How did God show His goodness to Naomi? How did her life change over the years?

Do you relate more to Ruth or Naomi? Why?

Applying Truth

Thinking back over the entire book of Ruth, what did you learn from Ruth's behavior?

Who did she want to follow first and foremost? What did you learn from the way she followed?

Was Ruth a blind follower? Explain your answer from the text.

How and when did she take initiative on her own?

Week Four: **Mentoring for the Long Haul, Part 2**

What about Naomi? What were some of her flaws? How did God use her to influence Ruth in spite of her shortcomings?

What was commendable about Naomi? What positive influence did she have on Ruth? (Look for specific instances since she operated differently at different times.)

@THE END OF THE DAY . . .

Ruth and Naomi's relationship is different from others in the Bible, but more like what we deal with every day. They weren't leaders like Moses and Joshua who had hundreds of thousands depending on them. They were normal people facing harder than normal life situations who learned to walk together in wisdom. As we close our time together this week, spend some quiet time in prayer asking God what specific truths from the account of Ruth and Naomi you can begin applying this week.

Week Four: **Mentoring for the Long Haul, Part 2**

Week Five
Mentoring in the Church

Be imitators of me [Paul], just as I also am of Christ.
—1 Corinthians 11:1

It's often said that imitation is the most sincere form of flattery, but is it more than this? Are mentoring and imitation related, and if so, how and for what purpose? What does God's Word have to say about imitating the lives of other people? Of those who have gone before us? And of God? This week we'll look at God's Word through the Apostle Paul and the author of the letter to the Hebrews to see what the Bible says about following the examples of others in the faith. We'll also consider the fine line between imitating people in their walk with God and idolizing them for their walk with God. This is, perhaps, a new phenomenon in our media-saturated, celebrity-driven culture, but we see flashes of it as far back as Peter and John, and Paul and Barnabas. There is nothing new under the sun.

Week Five: **Mentoring in the Church**

SETTING the SCENE...

Paul's letter to the Colossians focuses on the supremacy of Jesus Christ.

OBSERVE the TEXT of SCRIPTURE

READ Colossians 1:1-2, 28-29 and **CIRCLE** every reference to the author including pronouns.

Colossians 1:1-2, 28-29

1. *Paul, an apostle of Jesus Christ by the will of God, and Timothy our brother,*

2. *To the saints and faithful brethren in Christ who are at Colossae: Grace to you and peace from God our Father.*

28. *We proclaim Him [Christ], admonishing every man and teaching every man with all wisdom, so that we may present every man complete in Christ.*

29. *For this purpose also I labor, striving according to His power, which mightily works within me.*

DISCUSS with your group or PONDER on your own...

According to the text, who wrote Colossians?

What did the author do according to verse 28 and why?

According to verse 29, how did he characterize his actions?

Week Five: **Mentoring in the Church**

Digging Deeper

What is Paul praying for them?

If you've ever wondered what to pray for people the Bible has some great examples. There is a great one in the first few verses of Colossians. In Colossians 1:9-12 Paul told the Colossians exactly what he was praying for them:

> 9 For this reason also, since the day we heard of it, we have not ceased to pray for you and to ask that you may be filled with the knowledge of His will in all spiritual wisdom and understanding,
>
> 10 so that you will walk in a manner worthy of the Lord, to please Him in all respects, bearing fruit in every good work and increasing in the knowledge of God;
>
> 11 strengthened with all power, according to His glorious might, for the attaining of all steadfastness and patience; joyously
>
> 12 giving thanks to the Father, who has qualified us to share in the inheritance of the saints in Light.

Spend some time this week looking at what Paul specifically asks God for on behalf of the Colossian church and examine one, two, or more as you have the time and energy.

Once you have examined some of the phrases more closely, consider how more prayer in these areas would benefit the church as a whole.

Is there someone you should be praying these things for?

ONE STEP FURTHER:

Read the Letter to the Colossians

Whenever we look at verses from a book of the Bible, it's always best to get as much context as possible. If you have time this week, read through the letter to the Colossians. As you observe the text, notice what Paul says about Christ and how this relates to his desire to present every person "complete in Christ."

The whole book is only four chapters. All of them richly teach about Jesus Christ.

Record your observations below.

INFLUENCE
An Inductive Study on Mentoring

Week Five: **Mentoring in the Church**

How did he describe the power that fuels his labor?

> **FYI:**
>
> **Complete in Christ**
> In Colossians 1:28-29, Paul tells his readers exactly why he labors: "We proclaim Him [Jesus], admonishing every man and teaching every man with all wisdom, so that we may present every man complete in Christ. For this purpose also I labor, striving according to His power, which mightily works within me." The word translated *complete* is the Greek *telios*, which carries the idea of being full grown, mature, and lacking in no area. Very simply, Paul wanted to grow people up in the faith.

Do your life goals match those Paul had for believers in Jesus?

Do you concern yourself with being complete in Christ and helping to bring others to completion? If so, give some examples.

For what purpose do you labor in life? By what power do you do it?

Why do you do what you do? What empowers you?

Do you need to re-evaluate and re-set your priorities? How so?

If people are laboring to present you complete in Christ, do you think their job is easy or hard? Why?

INFLUENCE
An Inductive Study on Mentoring

Week Five: **Mentoring in the Church**

Paul says he labored to "present every man complete in Christ." What ramifications did that have on the people he labored for? Was there anything they needed to do to make the most of the time and energy Paul expended?

Is there anything you can do to make it easier for others to help you in your growing process?

Let's look at some more letters in Scripture—the first was written to a church in the Greek city of Corinth, the second to a church in Thessalonica.

SETTING the SCENE...

1 Corinthians is one of two letters Paul wrote to the Corinthians that are included in the New Testament. The church at Corinth had more than its share of problems including some severe moral issues Paul addressed head on.

OBSERVE the TEXT of SCRIPTURE

READ 1 Corinthians 11:1-2 and **CIRCLE** every reference to *Paul*. **BOX** in the word *imitators*.

1 Corinthians 11:1-2

1 *Be imitators of me [Paul], just as I also am of Christ.*

2 *Now I praise you because you remember me in everything and hold firmly to the traditions, just as I delivered them to you.*

READ the verses again and **UNDERLINE** every phrase that refers to actions that the church at Corinth is being instructed to do and/or is already doing.

Week Five: **Mentoring in the Church**

DISCUSS with your group or PONDER on your own . . .

How did Paul describe himself in verse 1?

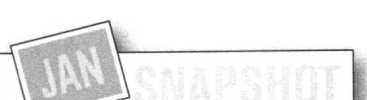

Why should I mentor?
It is foolish to waste things we've learned. There always will be those we walk ahead of who can have such a better trip if we "call back" to them and tell them what we've learned. It can save time, hurt and entanglements that are unnecessary. It is fun to know that something I've learned is helpful to someone else.

What did he call the church to do?

Why was this important?

What did Paul praise his readers for?

Paul exhorted his readers to imitate him as he imitated Christ. Can you could say this to someone with a clear conscience?

Why or why not?

Week Five: **Mentoring in the Church**

Digging Deeper

What are you looking for?

When we're looking for a mentor, it's important to keep our eyes opened and pay attention. But what are we looking *for?* This week, spend some time considering what biblical characteristics you are looking for in a mentor.

What biblical characters display traits you would want in a mentor? What are the traits?

What other specific characteristics are you looking for? Where in the Bible do you find this described?

What traits warn you to avoid a potential mentor? Why?

"This is my prayer for you . . . "

Shortly after I began a mentoring relationship with Deb back in the early 1990s she had me taking Precept Bible Studies. Our first class together was 2 Timothy, the second was Colossians. I still have a note she note me during the Colossians class that simply reads, "Colossians 1:9-12: This is my prayer for you."

She invested in me and she prayed for me. Whenever I come across that note and whenever I read Colossians 1 I'm reminded of how much the people of God need one another and I'm encouraged to be to other women what Deb has been to me.

INFLUENCE
An Inductive Study on Mentoring

Week Five: **Mentoring in the Church**

If not, what do you need to change to be able to say this?

It's Not About Making Clones and Drones

I think drones come from making it too personal. When a woman wants to be another me and not who God created her to be, it's really not a mentoring situation. If your mentee begins to dress like you, or pronounce words like you do, it might be wise to consider allowing someone else to mentor them.

SETTING the SCENE...

Paul wrote two letters to the Thessalonian church that are included in the New Testament. Unlike the Corinthians who had serious problems going on, the Thessalonians were commended for being imitators.

OBSERVE the TEXT of SCRIPTURE

READ 1 Thessalonians 1:1-10 and **CIRCLE** every reference to *Paul* and **UNDERLINE** every reference to the recipients.

1 Thessalonians 1:1-10

1. *Paul and Silvanus and Timothy, to the church of the Thessalonians in God the Father and the Lord Jesus Christ: Grace to you and peace.*

2. *We give thanks to God always for all of you, making mention of you in our prayers;*

3. *constantly bearing in mind your work of faith and labor of love and steadfastness of hope in our Lord Jesus Christ in the presence of our God and Father,*

4. *knowing, brethren beloved by God, His choice of you;*

5. *for our gospel did not come to you in word only, but also in power and in the Holy Spirit and with full conviction; just as you know what kind of men we proved to be among you for your sake.*

6. *You also became imitators of us and of the Lord, having received the word in much tribulation with the joy of the Holy Spirit,*

7. *so that you became an example to all the believers in Macedonia and in Achaia.*

8. *For the word of the Lord has sounded forth from you, not only in Macedonia and Achaia, but also in every place your faith toward God has gone forth, so that we have no need to say anything.*

9. *For they themselves report about us what kind of a reception we had with you, and how you turned to God from idols to serve a living and true God,*

10. *and to wait for His Son from heaven, whom He raised from the dead,* that is *Jesus, who rescues us from the wrath to come.*

READ the passage again, this time **BOX** in any references to *imitating* or being an *example*.

Week Five: **Mentoring in the Church**

DISCUSS with your group or PONDER on your own . . .

What did you learn by marking the recipients? To whom was Paul writing?

Based on verse 9, what were they doing before they received the Gospel that Paul brought?

According to 1 Thessalonians 1:3, what were Paul's readers' lives like after turning to God?

What specific characteristics did Paul note?

ONE STEP FURTHER:

Imitating Godly Character and Lifestyle

Think through some of the things you do that can benefit from observing and imitating godly behavior. I've started the list off with a few, but you can fill in some more including others you pick up this week.

How do I control my tongue?

How do I prioritize my marriage?

How do I deal with difficult people?

How do I . . .

How do I . . .

How do I . . .

INFLUENCE
An Inductive Study on Mentoring

Week Five: **Mentoring in the Church**

According to verse 6, what did Paul say they became? Who did they imitate?

Looking at verse 7, were they just imitators? What else did they become?

What brought about this life-change?

What came to them, was received, and then sounded forth?

How does your spiritual life compare to the Thessalonians'? How are you being changed and influencing others? Give some recent examples.

SETTING the SCENE...

The book of Hebrews teaches the supremacy of Jesus Christ above all things. After the author delivers a stern word about falling away from truth, he assures his readers he is convinced of better things concerning them.

ONE STEP FURTHER:

Read 1 Thessalonians
If you have time this week, check out the wider context. Record your findings below.

Week Five: **Mentoring in the Church**

OBSERVE the TEXT of SCRIPTURE

READ Hebrews 6:11-15 and **BOX** in every stated and implied directive the author makes.

Hebrews 6:11-15

11 And we desire that each one of you show the same diligence so as to realize the full assurance of hope until the end,

12 so that you will not be sluggish, but imitators of those who through faith and patience inherit the promises.

13 For when God made the promise to Abraham, since He could swear by no one greater, He swore by Himself,

14 saying, "I will surely bless you and I will surely multiply you."

15 And so, having patiently waited, he obtained the promise.

DISCUSS with your group or PONDER on your own . . .

What did the author want his readers to do and become according to verses 11 and 12?

How did the author of Hebrews describe people who inherit the promises? What do they display?

According to the text, what is the cure for sluggishness?

Consider your own spiritual life. What more aptly describes you—diligent or sluggish? Explain.

Running to the Front Row

In our celebrity-charged, people-worshipping world it's easy to get imitating behavior and character mixed up with idolizing personalities. "Groupies" aren't just a secular animal. The first time I encountered Christian groupies "up close and personal" was at a major conference for Christian women with open seating. I was with a group of seven women and volunteered to arrive when the doors opened to make sure we could all sit together.

What transpired one morning amazed me (and not good amazed)! Women were full-out sprinting for the seats at the front. Understand that the center had multiple jumbo screens throughout the building, so there was not a bad seat in the house and yet the running ensued and the line between godly imitating and idolizing became painfully evident.

That incident made me pay attention to that fine line people so easily slide across. It made me consider carefully both how I follow and lead.

Week Five: **Mentoring in the Church**

What specific steps can you take to become more diligent?

SETTING the SCENE...

As the writer of Hebrews finishes his letter, he gives some closing instructions.

OBSERVE the TEXT of SCRIPTURE

READ Hebrews 13:7 and **BOX** stated and implied instructions.

Hebrews 13:7

7   *Remember those who led you, who spoke the word of God to you; and considering the result of their conduct, imitate their faith.*

DISCUSS with your group or PONDER on your own...

What three directives did the author give?

According to Hebrews 13:7, whose faith should we imitate?

Why should we imitate their faith?

ONE STEP FURTHER:

Word Study: Imitators

If you have some extra time this week, find the Greek word translated *imitators* and see where else and how it is used in the New Testament. Record your findings below.

JAN SNAPSHOT

Living in the Church

Life in the church is sacred, wonderful, and sometimes a pain. Any time you are part of a group of people there will be "issues." That's what people bring to the table. If church leaders are unaware or inexperienced, the situation can create an issue of respect for those who are under their care. It is critical that mentors model respect for leaders to their mentees. If they don't the value of their mentoring will be compromised.

If a complaint about leadership comes up, it is right for the one who has a problem to go directly to the leader or leaders. It is not for mentors to discuss the complaint beyond the right thing to do about it.

INFLUENCE
An Inductive Study on Mentoring

Week Five: **Mentoring in the Church**

How does this biblical instruction differ from the way our self-made culture usually thinks?

What kind of responsibility does this place on church leadership? How should it be undertaken?

> ### ONE STEP FURTHER:
>
> **Word Studies: *Sluggish* and *Patiently Waited***
> If you have some time this week, look up the original words for *sluggish* and *patiently waited*. How are these words similar and different? What can you learn from each?

SETTING the SCENE...

Ephesians is another of Paul's letters. The "Therefore" that begins chapter 5 refers back to the content in 4 where Paul reminds his readers not to walk in their former manner of life but to put on the new self.

OBSERVE the TEXT of SCRIPTURE

READ Ephesians 5:1-4 and **BOX** commands and descriptions of imitators. **UNDERLINE** attitudes and behaviors that should *not* characterize Christ's followers.

Ephesians 5:1-4

1 Therefore be imitators of God, as beloved children;

2 and walk in love, just as Christ also loved you and gave Himself up for us, an offering and a sacrifice to God as a fragrant aroma.

3 But immorality or any impurity or greed must not even be named among you, as is proper among saints;

4 and there must be no filthiness and silly talk, or coarse jesting, which are not fitting, but rather giving of thanks.

Week Five: **Mentoring in the Church**

DISCUSS with your group or PONDER on your own . . .

According to verses 1 and 2, who did Paul tell his readers to imitate?

> **FYI:**
>
> **It's Easy to Catch Bad Behavior**
>
> *Do not be deceived: "Bad company corrupts good morals."*
> —1 Corinthians 15:33

Based on what you marked in verses 1 and 2, describe the characteristics of a person who imitates Christ.

List from verses 3 and 4 what should be absent from the lives of Christ's followers.

As you mature in Christ and help others grow, do you struggle with any of the sins listed? If so, does the text indicate a way to combat these choices and actions? How can you specifically apply this principle to your life?

@THE END OF THE DAY . . .

Godly examples spur us on in faith and help us learn better how to follow Christ. We should never blindly imitate but rather follow those who are exemplary followers of Christ, who point us to Him. Paul never purposed to make an army of "little Pauls"; his goal was to "present every man complete in Christ."

Let's face it, sometimes we need a picture. Godly mentors are living pictures, tangible examples of what it means to be "complete in Christ."

Mentoring Gone Wrong

Jehoash did right in the sight of the LORD all his days in which Jehoiada the priest instructed him.
— 2 Kings 12:2

Why is it that some of the best plans flop? We all have people who have disappointed us and most of us have disappointed a person or two ourselves. Sometimes the person is a relative who's strayed; other times it's a person we've invested our time, money, and/or energies in only to face the cold reality that something went wrong. The baton we've tried to pass has been bobbled, dropped, or flat out rejected. What then? What sense can we make of it? Are there any biblical precedents that shed light on these situations? This week we'll look at some notable failures in unlikely places.

Week Six: **Mentoring Gone Wrong**

DAVID AND SOLOMON

SETTING the SCENE...

In Psalm 27, a 14-verse psalm attributed to David, we see David both talking about God and praying to Him.

OBSERVE the TEXT of SCRIPTURE

READ Psalm 27:4, 7-8 and **UNDERLINE** every verb.

Psalm 27:4, 7-8

4   One thing I have asked from the LORD, that I shall seek:
    That I may dwell in the house of the LORD all the days of my life,

    To behold the beauty of the LORD
    And to meditate in His temple.

7   Hear, O LORD, when I cry with my voice,
    And be gracious to me and answer me.

8   When You said, "Seek My face," my heart said to You,
    "Your face, O LORD, I shall seek."

READ the passage again and **CIRCLE** every occurrence of the word *seek*.

DISCUSS with your group or PONDER on your own...

What did you learn about the author from marking the verbs in verse 4? What did he want to do and where did he want to be?

What did God tell him to do? How did he respond?

Week Six: **Mentoring Gone Wrong**

What can you say about David's heart from this text?

What one thing do you want from the Lord that you'll seek? How does your heart measure up? What correction does it need?

SETTING the SCENE...

The book of Proverbs is a collection of wise sayings, many attributed to Solomon.

OBSERVE the TEXT of SCRIPTURE

READ Proverbs 1:1 and Proverbs 4:3-4. **CIRCLE** every reference to the author including pronouns and **UNDERLINE** every reference to the author's father.

Proverbs 1:1

1 The proverbs of Solomon the son of David, king of Israel:

Proverbs 4:3-5

3 When I was a son to my father,
   Tender and the only son in the sight of my mother,

4 Then he taught me and said to me,
   "Let your heart hold fast my words;
   Keep my commandments and live..."

5 Acquire wisdom! Acquire understanding!
   Do not forget nor turn away from the words of my mouth.

Week Six: **Mentoring Gone Wrong**

DISCUSS with your group or PONDER on your own . . .

Who were the proverbs attributed to in this portion of the book of Proverbs? What position did he hold? Who was his father?

What did Solomon's father teach him?

What does the text tell us about his interaction with his father? Does the text hint at Solomon's age or David's way of teaching?

What advantage should this have given him in life?

Week Six: **Mentoring Gone Wrong**

SETTING the SCENE...

This incident takes place shortly after Solomon ascends the throne of Israel as king.

OBSERVE the TEXT of SCRIPTURE

READ 1 Kings 3:5-12 and **MARK** every reference to the words *ask* and *give*.

I Kings 3:5-12

5 In Gibeon the LORD appeared to Solomon in a dream at night; and God said, "Ask what you wish me to give you."

6 Then Solomon said, "You have shown great lovingkindness to Your servant David my father, according as he walked before You in truth and righteousness and uprightness of heart toward You; and You have reserved for him this great lovingkindness, that You have given him a son to sit on his throne, as it is this day.

7 "Now, O LORD my God, You have made Your servant king in place of my father David, yet I am but a little child; I do not know how to go out or come in.

8 "Your servant is in the midst of Your people which You have chosen, a great people who are too many to be numbered or counted.

9 "So give Your servant an understanding heart to judge Your people to discern between good and evil. For who is able to judge this great people of Yours?"

10 It was pleasing in the sight of the Lord that Solomon had asked this thing.

11 God said to him, "Because you have asked this thing and have not asked for yourself long life, nor have asked riches for yourself, nor have you asked for the life of your enemies, but have asked for yourself discernment to understand justice,

12 behold, I have done according to your words. Behold, I have given you a wise and discerning heart, so that there has been no one like you before you, nor shall one like you arise after you."

DISCUSS with your group or PONDER on your own...

What unique event occurred according to verse 5?

ONE STEP FURTHER:

Word Studies

What did David tell his son Solomon to seek? See what you can find out about the Hebrew words translated *wisdom* and *understanding* in Proverbs 4:5. Record your findings below. If you did the Digging Deeper in Week One, consider yourself done!

Week Six: **Mentoring Gone Wrong**

How did Solomon respond? What did he ask from God?

Was God pleased with his response? How do you know?

How did Solomon's request compare with his father's request?

What was the focus of each request?

Do you think one request was "better" than another? Why/why not?

On page 81 you were prompted to write something you'd like to ask of God. Why did you choose what did? Does your request align with Scripture?

ONE STEP FURTHER:

Psalm 27

If you have some extra time this week, read Psalm 27 in its entirety. What do we learn about David's life? What kind of situations did he face? What characterized his life? Record your observations on this Psalm below.

FYI:

Where It Begins

The fear of the LORD is the beginning of wisdom, And the knowledge of the Holy One is understanding.

—Proverbs 9:10

INFLUENCE
An Inductive Study on Mentoring

Week Six: **Mentoring Gone Wrong**

SETTING the SCENE...

As we pick up the story, Solomon is well established as king over all of Israel.

OBSERVE the TEXT of SCRIPTURE

READ I Kings 11:1-4; 9-10. **CIRCLE** every reference to *Solomon* and place a **TRIANGLE** over any references to *God*. As always be sure to mark pronouns as well.

I Kings 11:1-4, 9-10

1   Now King Solomon loved many foreign women along with the daughter of Pharaoh: Moabite, Ammonite, Edomite, Sidonian, and Hittite women,

2   from the nations concerning which the LORD had said to the sons of Israel, "You shall not associate with them, nor shall they associate with you, for they will surely turn your heart away after their gods." Solomon held fast to these in love.

3   He had seven hundred wives, princesses, and three hundred concubines, and his wives turned his heart away.

4   For when Solomon was old, his wives turned his heart away after other gods; and his heart was not wholly devoted to the LORD his God, as the heart of David his father had been.

9   Now the LORD was angry with Solomon because his heart was turned away from the LORD, the God of Israel, who had appeared to him twice,

10 and had commanded him concerning this thing, that he should not go after other gods; but he did not observe what the LORD had commanded.

READ the passage again, this time **UNDERLINE** every reference to the words *love* or *heart*.

Thoughts on Solomon: More than just knowing the truth...

Wisdom has to be received internally. You can know all the right answers and miss the truth a hundred miles. Finishing well is a determined pursuit. It doesn't "just happen" because you know the truth.

DISCUSS with your group or PONDER on your own...

What did you learn about Solomon's behavior?

What did you learn by marking references to God? What did God command in verse 2 and why?

INFLUENCE
An Inductive Study on Mentoring

Week Six: **Mentoring Gone Wrong**

What did you learn about Solomon's heart? What caused his condition?

How does Solomon's heart compare to David's?

Solomon chose foreign wives who opposed God. Are you entertaining sin in your life that stands in opposition to God? If so, what do you need to do? Why?

Does your heart look more like Solomon's or David's today? Explain.

What specific steps can you take toward having a whole heart for God?

What advantages did Solomon have?

How did he finish?

Week Six: **Mentoring Gone Wrong**

Digging Deeper

What went wrong with Solomon?

If you have some extra time this week, consider investigating how Solomon went wrong. Read through the entire account of his life. Watch for early warning signs like ungodly decisions that sent him off track. Record your observations below.

2 Samuel 5:13-16

2 Samuel 12:24-25

1 Kings 1–11

1 Chronicles 22–23:2

1 Chronicles 28–2 Chronicles 9

FYI:

Knowing What to Ask For

It must have been something for Solomon to be able to ask anything from God he wanted. Did you know God has said something very similar to us? In 1 John 5:13-15 we read these words penned by John the apostle, "These things I have written to you who believe in the name of the Son of God, so that you may know that you have eternal life. This is the confidence which we have before Him, that, if we ask anything according to His will, He hears us. And if we know that He hears us in whatever we ask, we know that we have the requests which we have asked from Him."

The better we get to know God's will through His Word and ask according to it the more we're assured He'll answer us.

Week Six: **Mentoring Gone Wrong**

JEHOIADA AND JOASH

SETTING the SCENE...

Jehoiada the priest and his wife Jehosheba saved their infant nephew, Joash, from his murderous grandmother who had all her grandsons who were heirs to the throne killed in her zealous grab for power. Jehoiada and his wife had baby Joash hidden until they were able to place him on the throne.

OBSERVE the TEXT of SCRIPTURE

READ 2 Chronicles 24:1-3. **CIRCLE** every reference to *Joash* and **UNDERLINE** every reference to
Jehoiada. As you read, also note references to time (e.g. *seven years old, all the days,* etc.).

2 Chronicles 24:1-3

1   *Joash* was *seven years old* when he became king, and he reigned *forty years* in Jerusalem; and his mother's name was *Zibiah* from *Beersheba.*

2   *Joash* did what was right in the sight of the LORD all the days of Jehoiada the priest.

3   Jehoiada took two wives for him, and he became the father of sons and daughters.

DISCUSS with your group or PONDER on your own...

Summarize everything you learned about Joash from the text.

Who was Jehoiada?

What did Joash do as long as Jehoiada was alive?

Week Six: **Mentoring Gone Wrong**

OBSERVE the TEXT of SCRIPTURE

READ 2 Chronicles 24:15-22. **CIRCLE** every reference to *Joash* and **UNDERLINE** every reference to *Jehoiada*. Again, watch for references to time.

2 Chronicles 24:15-22

15 Now when Jehoiada reached a ripe old age he died; he was one hundred and thirty years old at his death.

16 They buried him in the city of David among the kings, because he had done well in Israel and to God and His house.

17 But after the death of Jehoiada the officials of Judah came and bowed down to the king, and the king listened to them.

18 They abandoned the house of the LORD, the God of their fathers, and served the Asherim and the idols; so wrath came upon Judah and Jerusalem for this their guilt.

19 Yet He sent prophets to them to bring them back to the LORD; though they testified against them, they would not listen.

20 Then the Spirit of God came on Zechariah the son of Jehoiada the priest; and he stood above the people and said to them, "Thus God has said, 'Why do you transgress the commandments of the LORD and do not prosper? Because you have forsaken the LORD, He has also forsaken you.' "

21 So they conspired against him and at the command of the king they stoned him to death in the court of the house of the LORD.

22 Thus Joash the king did not remember the kindness which his father Jehoiada had shown him, but he murdered his son. And as he died he said, "May the LORD see and avenge!"

Kings and Chronicles
The books of Kings and Chronicles recount many of the same events but from different viewpoints.

DISCUSS with your group or PONDER on your own . . .

According to verses 17 and 18, what happened in the land of Judah after Jehoiada died?

What did Joash eventually do according to verse 22? What events led up to this behavior?

Week Six: **Mentoring Gone Wrong**

In hindsight, what corrective actions could Joash have taken to finish his life well?

If you are in a mentoring relationship (whether mentor or mentee), how can you guard against a "Joash outcome"? Explain.

Common Causes of Mentoring Failures

Mentoring usually fails where there are unmet expectations on either side. Paul and Barnabas fell apart when they disagreed about John Mark. (Isn't it interesting that it was over a mentee?) Their split was recorded for all time, even though Paul later asked for John Mark to come to him. Paul and Barnabas had different expectations for John Mark. This always causes problems.

I have found that mentoring works best when it "just happens." If there is a "certain mystery" as to how you have been brought together in a mentoring relationship, then it is probably a work of the Spirit. If all the "i's" have been dotted and "t's" have been crossed then there was probably too much humanity involved in it. The mark of God always leaves you with a little wonderment. The mark of man can probably be found in a printed syllabus somewhere.

JESUS AND JUDAS

OBSERVE the TEXT of SCRIPTURE

READ Matthew 10:1-4. **CIRCLE** every reference to *Jesus* and **UNDERLINE** the ones to *Judas*.

1   Jesus summoned His twelve disciples and gave them authority over unclean spirits, to cast them out, and to heal every kind of disease and every kind of sickness.

2   Now the names of the twelve apostles are these: The first, Simon, who is called Peter, and Andrew his brother; and James the son of Zebedee, and John his brother;

3   Philip and Bartholomew; Thomas and Matthew the tax collector; James the son of Alphaeus, and Thaddaeus;

4   Simon the Zealot, and Judas Iscariot, the one who betrayed Him.

DISCUSS with your group or PONDER on your own . . .

According to the text, what benefits did Judas have?

Week Six: **Mentoring Gone Wrong**

In spite of these benefits, what did Judas do?

The Works of Solomon
If you want to read the complete works of Solomon, check out Ecclesiastes, Song of Solomon, and Proverbs.

THE CURE

The kind of mentoring that matters is not just passing on knowledge or characteristics. It is not something a mentor can accomplish apart from the Holy Spirit's work and the participation of the person receiving instruction. Mentoring at its best is helping cultivate a heart condition that seeks God and clings to *Him*. David and Jehoiada cast the vision to those who followed but they had no power to make them receive it. Only God has the power to change a heart.

SETTING the SCENE . . .

In Jeremiah 13 God uses an object lesson to show the prophet Jeremiah the kind of relationship for which He had designed Israel and Judah.

OBSERVE the TEXT of SCRIPTURE

READ Jeremiah 13:11 and **CIRCLE** every occurrence of the word *cling*.

11 'For as the waistband clings to the waist of a man, so I made the whole household of Israel and the whole household of Judah cling to Me,' declares the LORD, 'that they might be for Me a people, for renown, for praise and for glory; but they did not listen.'

DISCUSS with your group or PONDER on your own . . .

According to the text, what was God's purpose for Israel and Judah? What picture did He use?

Week Six: **Mentoring Gone Wrong**

Did Israel and Judah act consistently with God's purpose? How do the ideas of remnant and Paul's Israel within Israel help explain what happened? (See Romans 9:6-8; 11:5-7.)

Different Spellings to Watch For

As you read different accounts in the Old Testament, you'll sometimes run across slightly different spellings of names. "Joash," for instance, is "Jehoash" in 2 Kings, same guy, different spelling. Before you get irritated, remember we do it too. My husband is Dave or David on any given day, my son, Brad, Bradley, or simply B.

Does the Church cling to God the way a waistband clings to the waist of a man? Do you cling to God?

Sometimes it Works . . . Sometimes it Fades

Mentoring works when it works. When it doesn't, it usually just fades away. In my experience, good mentoring happens when God has brought together two people. It isn't a relationship that can be successfully assigned or programmed. It's totally a work of the Spirit.

What did Solomon cling to? What did Joash cling to? How did their choices turn out?

Are you clinging to anything with the vigor that belongs to God alone? If so, what is it? What do you need to do about it?

Week Six: **Mentoring Gone Wrong**

SETTING the SCENE . . .

Psalm 63 is attributed to David. Some think he is in the wilderness of Judah fleeing from his son Absalom who is attempting a coup.

OBSERVE the TEXT of SCRIPTURE

READ Psalm 63:6-8 and **CIRCLE** every reference to *David*. **UNDERLINE** verbs that indicate what he did.

6   When I remember You on my bed,
    I meditate on You in the night watches,

7   For You have been my help,
    And in the shadow of Your wings I sing for joy.

8   My soul clings to You;
    Your right hand upholds me.

READ the text again and **BOX** every action attributed to *God*.

DISCUSS with your group or PONDER on your own . . .

As we close our time today, let's look again at some of David's behaviors. What do you see David doing in this text? How does this contrast with his son Solomon's behaviors?

What did God do for David?

When did David remember and meditate?

Dealing with Mentoring Failures

If it's not working, gently call it quits. It will give both of you relief.

If co-dependency has entered the picture, it can be more painful to continue than to quit. Be aware that demands, hurts, slights and jealousies are all marks of dependencies. Before you even begin a mentoring relationship, it is wise to understand what co-dependency is. It happens between the weak and strong and is an arrangement where one is controlling the other.

For more information on co-dependency—what it is and how to avoid it—check out Jan's book, *Please Don't Say You Need Me*.

www.jansilvious.com/book.html

Week Six: **Mentoring Gone Wrong**

Is your life characterized by remembering, meditating, singing, and clinging? If not, how can you begin to incorporate David's actions into your life?

> **FYI:**
>
> **Family Connections**
> In killing Jehoiada's son Zechariah, King Joash not only forgot the kindness Jehoiada had shown him but also killed off his own first cousin. (Joash's father, King Ahaziah, and Zechariah's mother, Jehoshabeath, were siblings: 2 Chronicles 22:10.)

@THE END OF THE DAY . . .

Like it or not, not every mentoring relationship ends as what we'd consider a smashing success. What we would consider "bad outcomes" touched not only King David and his son Solomon (the wisest man in history), the godly priest Jehoiada and King Joash, but even Jesus in His dealings with Judas. Sometimes we fail to begin because we fear we might fail, but we can't let that stop us. It didn't stop David, it didn't stop Jesus, nor should it stop us from seeking to help others learn to cling to God above all else.

Week Seven
The Mentoring of the Spirit and the Word

Your testimonies also are my delight;
They are *my counselors.*
– Psalm 119:24

In times past, God's people did not have God's Word available to them as we do today. Some lived before any of it had been recorded, others when only parts of it had been written down, still others before it was translated into their local language, but never in history has God's complete written Word been as accessible in its fullness to the masses as it is today. Not only that but during Old Testament times the Holy Spirit came upon certain people for certain tasks from time to time. Now, though, the Spirit permanently indwells *all* believers guiding them into all truth. While human mentors can help us grow, our greatest need is the Spirit and Word's mentoring to learn to follow Jesus and feed ourselves. We don't want to risk becoming like King Joash or the people during the time of the judges who did well only as long as the mentors of their days were alive. This week we'll consider what following Jesus and being mentored by the Spirit through the Word mean.

Warning Sign
Telling too much too soon is a boundary issue. Inappropriate sharing without mutual trust is a danger sign. Jealousy of other relationships is a big warning sign. Personal information that is not kept personal is the biggest issue of all. The mentoring relationship does not extend to spouses. What is shared in the context of the mentoring relationship stays there.

Week Seven: **The Mentoring of the Spirit and the Word**

THE TWELVE

SETTING the SCENE...

Each of the following accounts takes place early in Jesus' ministry as He calls His disciples.

FYI:

What is Your God?

"Whatever your heart clings to and confides in, that is really your God."
—Martin Luther

OBSERVE the TEXT of SCRIPTURE

READ the following texts and **MARK** every reference to *Jesus* with a cross. **CIRCLE** every occurrence of the word *follow*.

Matthew 4:18-20

18 Now as Jesus was walking by the Sea of Galilee, He saw two brothers, Simon who was called Peter, and Andrew his brother, casting a net into the sea; for they were fishermen.

19 And He said to them, "Follow Me, and I will make you fishers of men."

20 Immediately they left their nets and followed Him.

Matthew 9:9

9 As Jesus went on from there, He saw a man called Matthew, sitting in the tax collector's booth; and He said to him, "Follow Me!" And he got up and followed Him.

DISCUSS with your group or PONDER on your own...

What were these men doing when Jesus came?

What did Jesus say to them?

How did the men respond?

Week Seven: **The Mentoring of the Spirit and the Word**

How quickly did they respond? What did they leave behind?

SETTING the SCENE...

While the previous events took place at the beginning of Jesus' ministry, the following conversation between Jesus and Peter takes place after He has been raised from the dead.

OBSERVE the TEXT of SCRIPTURE

READ John 21:18-22 and **UNDERLINE** every reference to *Peter*. **CIRCLE** every occurrence of the phrase *follow Me*.

John 21:18-22

18 *"Truly, truly, I say to you, when you were younger, you used to gird yourself and walk wherever you wished; but when you grow old, you will stretch out your hands and someone else will gird you, and bring you where you do not wish to go."*

19 *Now this He said, signifying by what kind of death he would glorify God. And when He had spoken this, He said to him, "Follow Me!"*

20 *Peter, turning around, saw the disciple whom Jesus loved following them; the one who also had leaned back on His bosom at the supper and said, "Lord, who is the one who betrays You?"*

21 *So Peter seeing him said to Jesus, "Lord, and what about this man?"*

22 *Jesus said to him, "If I want him to remain until I come, what is that to you? You follow Me!"*

DISCUSS with your group or PONDER on your own...

What did you learn from marking Peter in the text? How was he going to die?

Week Seven: **The Mentoring of the Spirit and the Word**

What did Jesus command Peter in verse 19?

According to verses 20-21, how did Peter respond to the news and the command?

What point did Jesus make in verse 22?

Do your eyes ever wander off Jesus as Peter's eyes wandered, wondering what God has in store for others instead of focusing on Him alone? How can you increase your focus?

THE OTHERS

SETTING the SCENE...

Speaking to a group of Jewish people, Jesus talks about Himself, His sheep, and His Father.

Week Seven: **The Mentoring of the Spirit and the Word**

OBSERVE the TEXT of SCRIPTURE

READ John 10:27-30 and **CIRCLE** the word *follow*. **UNDERLINE** every reference to *sheep* including pronouns.

John 10:27-30

27 "My sheep hear My voice, and I know them, and they follow Me;

28 and I give eternal life to them, and they will never perish; and no one will snatch them out of My hand.

29 "My Father, who has given them to Me, is greater than all; and no one is able to snatch them out of the Father's hand.

30 "I and the Father are one."

DISCUSS with your group or PONDER on your own . . .

According to the text, what will Jesus' sheep do?

How does this compare with what they do according to texts we've already looked at?

What relationship do Jesus' sheep have to the Father? Explain.

What assurances does the text give? How can these truths affect thinking and behavior?

ONE STEP FURTHER:

How do we follow Jesus?
When Jesus calls people to follow Him, what is He asking? Spend some time this week exploring Greek words for *follow*. Also look at the contexts of this call. Record your observations below.

Week Seven: **The Mentoring of the Spirit and the Word**

SETTING the SCENE...

John 16 falls into a section of Scripture called The Upper Room Discourse, the last address Jesus makes to His disciples before He's handed over to Jewish leaders on the way to the cross.

> **FYI:**
>
> **The Disciple Jesus Loved**
> Although "the disciple that Jesus loved" is not named, many believe he's John the Apostle, author of the fourth Gospel, three letters (1, 2, and 3 John) and Revelation.

OBSERVE the TEXT of SCRIPTURE

READ John 16:5-7, 13-15 and **MARK** every reference to *Jesus* (who is speaking in the text) with a cross. **CIRCLE** every reference to the *Holy Spirit*, and **MARK** references to *God the Father* with a **TRIANGLE**.

John 16:5-7

5 "But now I am going to Him who sent Me; and none of you asks Me, 'Where are You going?'

6 "But because I have said these things to you, sorrow has filled your heart.

7 "But I tell you the truth, it is to your advantage that I go away; for if I do not go away, the Helper will not come to you; but if I go, I will send Him to you.

John 16:13-15

13 "But when He, the Spirit of truth, comes, He will guide you into all the truth; for He will not speak on His own initiative, but whatever He hears, He will speak; and He will disclose to you what is to come.

14 "He will glorify Me, for He will take of Mine and will disclose it to you.

15 "All things that the Father has are Mine; therefore I said that He takes of Mine and will disclose it to you."

DISCUSS with your group or PONDER on your own...

What is the main topic of these passages? Where and to whom was Jesus going?

What was the disciples' emotional condition? Explain.

Week Seven: **The Mentoring of the Spirit and the Word**

How was it to the disciples' advantage that Jesus went away? Who would He send to them?

What is the Helper called in verse 13? What will He do according to verses 13 and 14?

Do you approach the Word of God believing the Spirit of truth will guide you into all truth? Why or why not?

How can your life change if you appropriate and apply this truth more fully?

SETTING the SCENE...

John 17 is commonly referred to as the High Priestly Prayer. Jesus prays for His disciples just prior to going to the cross.

"Lord, and what about this man?"

One of the most satisfying and restful answers to "What about him?" or "Why does she get to do what I want to do?" comes from 1 Corinthians 12:4-6: "Now there are varieties of gifts, but the same Spirit. And there are varieties of ministries, and the same Lord. There are varieties of effects, but the same God who works all things in all persons."

I've always summed it up this way: "God gives the gift, God gives the ministry, God gives the result." That's where you leave it and then you can be and do what God intends.

It's Not a Suggestion

When Jesus says to Peter, "Follow Me," He uses a Greek imperative verb meaning a command, not a suggestion. You don't need to be a Greek expert to use Greek study tools. In fact, for a quick overview of how to do a word study in the Greek New Testament or Hebrew Old Testament, pick up a copy of *The New How to Study Your Bible*. It's easier than you'd think!

Week Seven: **The Mentoring of the Spirit and the Word**

OBSERVE the TEXT of SCRIPTURE

READ John 17:14-21 and **CIRCLE** every reference to *word* and *truth*. **UNDERLINE** every reference to *sanctification*.

John 17:14-21

14 "I have given them Your word; and the world has hated them, because they are not of the world, even as I am not of the world.

15 "I do not ask You to take them out of the world, but to keep them from the evil one.

16 "They are not of the world, even as I am not of the world.

17 "Sanctify them in the truth; Your word is truth.

18 "As You sent Me into the world, I also have sent them into the world.

19 "For their sakes I sanctify Myself, that they themselves also may be sanctified in truth.

20 "I do not ask on behalf of these alone, but for those also who believe in Me through their word;

21 that they may all be one; even as You, Father, are in Me and I in You, that they also may be in Us, so that the world may believe that You sent Me."

DISCUSS with your group or PONDER on your own . . .

In John 16, Jesus told His disciples that the Spirit will guide them into all truth. In John 17, how did Jesus define truth?

Briefly list everything you've learned in this text about the *word* and *truth*.

Does this text apply only to the disciples Jesus originally spoke to? Why or why not?

How do you keep focus?
I have drifted a time or two or three but God has always been faithful to bring me back. That's His business. Mine is to remember that He called me to what I'm doing and I need to trust Him with all the results. I don't believe my own press. That can be very deceiving. People who do invariably wander farther than they ever intended.

Week Seven: **The Mentoring of the Spirit and the Word**

Based on the texts we've examined so far, how can you follow Jesus today? Explain.

What result(s) was Jesus looking for then and now? Explain.

The Work of the Spirit

I have benefited from a string of godly influences and mentors but nothing has changed me like the Word of God itself. The Spirit drew me to the Word in the first place. Don't get me wrong, I grew up understanding the importance of being in the Word but it wasn't until the Spirit Himself convicted me of the need and gave me the power to obey that my life started to radically change. People have encouraged me, but God has changed me.

Digging Deeper

A Hunt for Dead Mentors

The older we get, the harder it becomes to find people who have walked with God longer and who have more life experience than we have. But many great mentors live on through books. This week take some time to research and ask around about godly men and women of faith you can learn from who recorded their thoughts on paper. I'll give you some categories to think about for a starting point.

Biographies:

Authors suggested by wise friends:

Classic Christian thinkers:

Others:

INFLUENCE
An Inductive Study on Mentoring

Week Seven: **The Mentoring of the Spirit and the Word**

SETTING the SCENE...

Psalm 119 is a 22-stanza acrostic poem about what God's Word is and does. Although we don't know for sure who wrote it, David is one of the possible authors.

The Mentoring of the Word in My Life

I usually am gripped by words and phrases rather than whole passages when the Lord teaches me something in the Word. I can read and read and then the Spirit will grasp a phrase and press it into my heart as if to say, "Pay attention. You'll need this!" I love this relationship. I may not have even a clue about something I need to learn and there it will be, right in the Word. The Holy Spirit is my "mentor" to lead me into all truth.

OBSERVE the TEXT of SCRIPTURE

READ Psalm 119:17-24 and **CIRCLE** every reference to God's *word* including synonyms (e.g. *word, law, commandment, precepts, testimonies*, etc.).

17 Deal bountifully with Your servant,
    That I may live and keep Your word.

18 Open my eyes, that I may behold
    Wonderful things from Your law.

19 I am a stranger in the earth;
    Do not hide Your commandments from me.

20 My soul is crushed with longing
    After Your ordinances at all times.

21 You rebuke the arrogant, the cursed,
    Who wander from Your commandments.

22 Take away reproach and contempt from me,
    For I observe Your testimonies.

23 Even though princes sit and talk against me,
    Your servant meditates on Your statutes.

24 Your testimonies also are my delight;
    They are my counselors.

DISCUSS with your group or PONDER on your own...

What did the psalmist ask God for in verses 17-20?

Week Seven: **The Mentoring of the Spirit and the Word**

What is the psalmist's attitude toward the Word of God throughout this stanza?

How did he characterize God's words in verse 24? What were they to him? How true is this in your life?

Do people you seek counsel from point you back to God's Word? When you give counsel, do you point people to truths and principles from God's Word? Explain.

OBSERVE the TEXT of SCRIPTURE

READ Psalm 119:97-104 and again circle every reference to God's *word* including synonyms.

97 O how I love Your law!
    It is my meditation all the day.

98 Your commandments make me wiser than my enemies,
    For they are ever mine.

99 I have more insight than all my teachers,
    For Your testimonies are my meditation.

100 I understand more than the aged,
    Because I have observed Your precepts.

101 I have restrained my feet from every evil way,
    That I may keep Your word.

102 I have not turned aside from Your ordinances,
    For You Yourself have taught me.

103 How sweet are Your words to my taste!
    Yes, sweeter than honey to my mouth!

104 From Your precepts I get understanding;
    Therefore I hate every false way.

Week Seven: **The Mentoring of the Spirit and the Word**

DISCUSS with your group or PONDER on your own . . .

What was the psalmist's attitude towards God's law in verse 97?

How did God's words benefit him according to verses 98-100?

Who did he say had been his teacher in verse 102?

What other benefits did he note in the remainder of the stanza?

Have God's Words increased your wisdom, insight, and understanding? If not, why not?

How did the psalmist participate in the Word? What can you learn from his posture toward the Word of God?

Week Seven: **The Mentoring of the Spirit and the Word**

Are the words of God sweeter than honey to your mouth today? Sweeter than chocolate?

@THE END OF THE DAY . . .

As you close out your time of study this week, consider whether you rely more heavily on God's Word or man's. Don't gloss over this question. If you do rely more heavily on people, are they people who point you to God? Are they people who help you learn to seek Him for yourself and teach you how to pass on what you learn to others?

Week Seven: **The Mentoring of the Spirit and the Word**

Week Eight
Empowering Your Legacy

*But you, be sober in all things, endure hardship,
do the work of an evangelist, fulfill your ministry.*
— Paul's Words to Timothy in 2 Timothy 4:5

Some people live to build monuments to self. Christ's calling is far higher. None of us will live forever in this world. Our mortal years will come to an end either later or sooner. So an important question is: *Are you equipping people to come behind you?* Are you investing in and empowering the people who will outlive you? Are you carefully passing along not only the truth you've learned but also the wisdom that comes after years of walking with God? We've talked a lot about being wise observers, about paying attention, about being the follower. But we also need to think about being the leader and intentionally passing on what has been entrusted to us. This week we're going to focus on Paul's last words to his child in the faith, Timothy. As we do we'll observe, among other things, *why* his words to this young man carry weight, *how* he speaks to Timothy, and *what* he feels compelled to pass on as his life draws to a close.

Godly Dead Mentors Live On

"He is no fool who gives what he cannot keep to gain that which he cannot lose." Jim Elliott died at the hands of South American Indians in 1956 yet his words have inspired countless people to follow God fully. As the author of Hebrews said of Abel, "though he is dead, he still speaks" (Hebrews 11:4b).

INFLUENCE
An Inductive Study on Mentoring

Week Eight: **Empowering Your Legacy**

OBSERVE the TEXT of SCRIPTURE

READ 2 Timothy 1:1-14 and **CIRCLE** every reference to *Paul*. **UNDERLINE** every reference to *Timothy*. Don't forget to mark the pronouns.

2 Timothy 1:1-14

1 Paul, an apostle of Christ Jesus by the will of God, according to the promise of life in Christ Jesus,

2 To Timothy, my beloved son: Grace, mercy and peace from God the Father and Christ Jesus our Lord.

3 I thank God, whom I serve with a clear conscience the way my forefathers did, as I constantly remember you in my prayers night and day,

4 longing to see you, even as I recall your tears, so that I may be filled with joy.

5 For I am mindful of the sincere faith within you, which first dwelt in your grandmother Lois and your mother Eunice, and I am sure that it is *in you* as well.

6 For this reason I remind you to kindle afresh the gift of God which is in you through the laying on of my hands.

7 For God has not given us a spirit of timidity, but of power and love and discipline.

8 Therefore do not be ashamed of the testimony of our Lord or of me His prisoner, but join with me in suffering for the gospel according to the power of God,

9 who has saved us and called us with a holy calling, not according to our works, but according to His own purpose and grace which was granted us in Christ Jesus from all eternity,

10 but now has been revealed by the appearing of our Savior Christ Jesus, who abolished death and brought life and immortality to light through the gospel,

11 for which I was appointed a preacher and an apostle and a teacher.

12 For this reason I also suffer these things, but I am not ashamed; for I know whom I have believed and I am convinced that He is able to guard what I have entrusted to Him until that day.

13 Retain the standard of sound words which you have heard from me, in the faith and love which are in Christ Jesus.

14 Guard, through the Holy Spirit who dwells in us, the treasure which has been entrusted to you.

The Mentoring of Dead Mentors

Amy Carmichael is a woman who had great passion, lived her life with purpose, and had the good sense to write, write, write. After she could no longer be about her work of rescuing children from temple prostitution, she wrote prolifically to the young people who had served alongside her at the Donavur Fellowship. Not only did she teach them in her letters, she also left a legacy of wonderful insights and deep probing thoughts for those of us who came along later. I recommend her writings to anyone who wants to be mentored by a godly and very savvy woman. She was unique. She thought "out of the box." That's one of the things I love about her—her insights were always fresh and unexpected. She taught me to love the Lord and to relax in His love.

Week Eight: **Empowering Your Legacy**

DISCUSS with your group or PONDER on your own . . .

How did Paul refer to Timothy? What did he know about Timothy? Do you think this was a close relationship? Why/why not?

How did Paul describe himself?

How did Paul's mission overlap Timothy's?

What specific instructions did Paul give to Timothy in this section? How would they help when Timothy carried on in Paul's absence?

If you were losing a mentor, what kind of words would you want to hear?

INFLUENCE
An Inductive Study on Mentoring

Week Eight: **Empowering Your Legacy**

Digging Deeper

Different Words at Different Times of Life

While we're focusing on 2 Timothy in the main portion of our lesson, it's obvious that it is the second part of a set. If you have some time this week, read 1 and 2 Timothy and observe the different subjects Paul addresses to Timothy at different stages of their time together.

The focus of 1 Timothy . . . .

The focus of 2 Timothy . . .

Take some time to compare and contrast the content as well as the tone of the letters.

What was the most interesting/applicable truth you discovered and why?

Week Eight: **Empowering Your Legacy**

OBSERVE the TEXT of SCRIPTURE

READ the selections from 2 Timothy 2 below. **UNDERLINE** everything Timothy is supposed to do. **CIRCLE** everything he is supposed to avoid.

2 Timothy 2:1-4, 14-15, 22-26

1 You therefore, my son, be strong in the grace that is in Christ Jesus.

2 The things which you have heard from me in the presence of many witnesses, entrust these to faithful men who will be able to teach others also.

3 Suffer hardship with me, as a good soldier of Christ Jesus.

4 No soldier in active service entangles himself in the affairs of everyday life, so that he may please the one who enlisted him as a soldier.

14 Remind them of these things, and solemnly charge them in the presence of God not to wrangle about words, which is useless and leads to the ruin of the hearers.

15 Be diligent to present yourself approved to God as a workman who does not need to be ashamed, accurately handling the word of truth.

22 Now flee from youthful lusts and pursue righteousness, faith, love and peace, with those who call on the Lord from a pure heart.

23 But refuse foolish and ignorant speculations, knowing that they produce quarrels.

24 The Lord's bond-servant must not be quarrelsome, but be kind to all, able to teach, patient when wronged,

25 with gentleness correcting those who are in opposition, if perhaps God may grant them repentance leading to the knowledge of the truth,

26 and they may come to their senses and escape from the snare of the devil, having been held captive by him to do his will.

Why Legacy is Important
I don't want to leave this earth without a trace. God has me here for this time for His purpose. Failure to pass this on to the next generation leaves them wondering whether or not they're here for a purpose. God has a plan and He's called me to tell it.

DISCUSS with your group or PONDER on your own . . .

What specific instructions did Paul give Timothy?

Week Eight: **Empowering Your Legacy**

What was he to avoid or flee?

Which of these instructions can we apply today? How will learning to, say, not wrangle about words affect us and others as we live as bond-servants of Christ?

Which of Paul's words address areas of temptation or sin you struggle with?

How can you apply this distant mentor's words this week?

Do you see any common themes in his exhortations?

Week Eight: **Empowering Your Legacy**

OBSERVE the TEXT of SCRIPTURE

READ the excerpts from 2 Timothy 3 and 4 below. Again, **UNDERLINE** every instruction and exhortation Paul gives to Timothy. **BOX** every warning about coming wickedness Timothy can expect.

2 Timothy 3:10-17

10 Now you followed my teaching, conduct, purpose, faith, patience, love, perseverance,

11 persecutions, and sufferings, such as happened to me at Antioch, at Iconium and at Lystra; what persecutions I endured, and out of them all the Lord rescued me!

12 Indeed, all who desire to live godly in Christ Jesus will be persecuted.

13 But evil men and impostors will proceed from bad to worse, deceiving and being deceived.

14 You, however, continue in the things you have learned and become convinced of, knowing from whom you have learned them,

15 and that from childhood you have known the sacred writings which are able to give you the wisdom that leads to salvation through faith which is in Christ Jesus.

16 All Scripture is inspired by God and profitable for teaching, for reproof, for correction, for training in righteousness;

17 so that the man of God may be adequate, equipped for every good work.

2 Timothy 4:1-8

1 I solemnly charge you in the presence of God and of Christ Jesus, who is to judge the living and the dead, and by His appearing and His kingdom:

2 preach the word; be ready in season and out of season; reprove, rebuke, exhort, with great patience and instruction.

3 For the time will come when they will not endure sound doctrine; but wanting to have their ears tickled, they will accumulate for themselves teachers in accordance to their own desires,

4 and will turn away their ears from the truth and will turn aside to myths.

5 But you, be sober in all things, endure hardship, do the work of an evangelist, fulfill your ministry.

6 For I am already being poured out as a drink offering, and the time of my departure has come.

7 I have fought the good fight, I have finished the course, I have kept the faith;

8 in the future there is laid up for me the crown of righteousness, which the Lord, the righteous Judge, will award to me on that day; and not only to me, but also to all who have loved His appearing.

Rev. Walter Olson, aka Grandpa

Two years ago my son Brad and I started taking Hebrew classes together. He wanted to learn the language after we returned from a trip to Israel. That was a good enough for me but I had a reason of my own. When I was taking Greek during my time at Wheaton College, my Grandpa would often tell me, "Pam, one day you need to study Hebrew, too." He was never overbearing, always spoke with a twinkle in his eye, but he did put it into words.

I'm still a long way from being able to handle the language adequately, but I keep working at it and will continue for the rest of my life because my Grandpa planted a seed. I know I am part of his legacy and if he thought it was important for me to know Hebrew, well, I'm going to know Hebrew. If he hadn't encouraged me, I wouldn't have taken the plunge. It's that simple.

Week Eight: **Empowering Your Legacy**

DISCUSS with your group or PONDER on your own . . .

What did Paul warn Timothy about? Are these warnings applicable to us today? If so, how can you apply them in your life this week?

How do you typically respond to warnings? Do you pay attention or ignore them? Does your response depend on *who* warns? Explain.

Based on these texts and the ones we have looked at earlier in the lesson, what kind of example did Paul provide? Specifically, what kind of life did he live after Christ revealed Himself to him?

Should we weigh peoples' actions before following their teachings and heeding their warnings? Why or why not?

FYI:

Background on 2 Timothy
Scholars agree that 2 Timothy is the last letter Paul wrote before he died at the hands of the Roman government. So in this letter we have his last words to Timothy, his dear son in the faith and co-worker in the cause of the Gospel of Jesus Christ.

INFLUENCE
An Inductive Study on Mentoring

Week Eight: **Empowering Your Legacy**

Digging Deeper

Other Famous Last Words

We've looked at Paul's last words to Timothy and later in the lesson we'll have a chance to look at Jesus' last words. While the words of Paul and Jesus are both *extremely* significant, they aren't the only "famous last words" in Scripture. With your extra time this week, think through significant last words (forceful, valuable, memorable) from other biblical figures and consider how you can apply what you learn from them.

How do you get there? Well, let's look at a couple of different routes. One is to simply think through the biblical story. This only works if you are familiar with most of the Bible. Trace in your mind people of significance whose stories you remember. As I think through the story of Scripture, certain figures come to mind as having "last words" that would be reasonably easy to locate: Moses and Joshua are a couple of good ones to start off with.

Another way to locate this information is to run concordance searches with "end of life" terminology. Search on *died, rested with his fathers, buried,* and *slept* for starters. Searching on words like these will bring you to potential places of interest.

ONE STEP FURTHER:

Whose legacy are YOU?
Spend a little time this week considering the people who consider *you* to be part of *their* legacy. Record their names below along with what they have passed on to you about God. How did God use their part in the family tree of faith to directly impact you?

INFLUENCE
An Inductive Study on Mentoring

Week Eight: **Empowering Your Legacy**

Has anyone passed God's commands and warnings to you as Paul did to Timothy? If so, how did it impact you? Did you rise to the call?

Are you living in integrity so you can call back to those who are following you with warnings and instructions and expect to be heard?

Do you think Paul gave Timothy enough information to run with the baton? Why/why not?

Who are some of the "Pauls" in your life?

How about "Timothys"?

What do you want your legacy to be? Does your life show it?

Legacies I'm part of . . .

Do you ever sit back and think about whose legacies you're part of? Most of us are part of our parents legacies. I'll carry on the legacies of both of my parents but also those of other godly people who influenced me and whose godly labor will live on in me after they are gone.

Immanuel Church has been in existence since 1895. The building has moved three times over the course of its years, but the church has continued. I am part of that legacy.

I'm part of the legacy of AWANA Clubs International. Can't say I memorized for pure reasons, but I learned my verses and I loved to run the circles.

I am part of the legacy of Wheaton College. I'm no Billy Graham or Jim Elliott, but what I learned at Wheaton shaped who I am and how I interact with my world.

I am part of the legacy of Precept Ministries International and Kay Arthur.

I'm part of the legacies of other individuals who have invested in me over the years — Jan Silvious, Jan Priddy, Debbie Boerman, and plenty of others.

None of these tried to point me to themselves—each faithfully pointed me to God and His Word. My parents taught me to *love God* and brought me to a church that *loves God and loves people.* Awana taught me to *love God's Word* and *share the good news* with others. At Wheaton I learned to *think biblically* and live as the motto says *For Christ and His Kingdom.*

People and organizations who leave godly legacies aren't building monuments to themselves. They're investing their lives in people and pointing them back to God!

INFLUENCE
An Inductive Study on Mentoring

Week Eight: **Empowering Your Legacy**

Digging Deeper

The Last Words of Jesus

Last words are important. If you have some extra time this week, consider the last words of Jesus. We actually have multiple places we can look depending on how you want to define "last words." Today, let's read carefully through Jesus' final teaching to His disciples before going to the cross in John 13–16 (often referred to as the Upper Room Discourse), His prayer in John 17 (sometimes called The High Priestly Prayer), and the last words of the risen Christ before He ascends to heaven as recorded by Luke in Acts. If you have more time, go ahead and think through some of the more informal comments Jesus made during His final hours on earth. As you read, record your observations below.

John 13–17

Acts 1:4-8

The Most Important Thing I'm Passing On

I think one of the most important things I am passing on is my belief that life with the Lord is an adventure.

It is my journey with God, so every day has a certain mystery about it that I love to embrace. I want those who come behind me to find that adventure in their own lives. Whether they are living good days or bad days, I want those I influence to know that they can know the truth of Psalm 91:1: "He who dwells in the shelter of the Most High will abide under the shadow of the Almighty." In that shelter and under that shadow, there is a life of "deep knowing" that takes us through life with confidence that there are purposes beyond our own.

An equal "most important thing" is "Always ask, 'Where is it written?'" Don't believe anything just because you've been told it. Instead, make it a point to *know* "where it is written!" If it is important, God included it in His Word. If it is not, you don't have to worry about it.

Finally, and of equal importance to the first two: God's love is without bounds. Whatever you believe, be sure you don't forget that underlying all that happens, God loves you dearly.

INFLUENCE
An Inductive Study on Mentoring

Week Eight: **Empowering Your Legacy**

@THE END OF THE DAY . . .

Before you close the final page of this study, spend some time quiet time with God and consider the most significant truth He has taught you through His Word. What steps will you take with the truth you now have? Is it time to look for a mentor or to make yourself available to share what you've learned with someone else? Maybe it's time for both as there is always more to learn and there is always something to pass along.

The power of encouragement . . .
A mentor is an "encourager," plain and simple. If you can't encourage, don't mentor.

Week Eight: **Empowering Your Legacy**

While it is tempting for me as a teacher and writer to give you my words and try to tie this study up in a fancy little package, as we close I want to leave you with some of my favorite words from Scripture—words that are living and active and sharper than any two-edged sword—and which I believe embody and capsulize so much of what we have learned these past weeks.

Hebrews 12:1-3

1. *Therefore, since we have so great a cloud of witnesses surrounding us, let us also lay aside every encumbrance and the sin which so easily entangles us, and let us run with endurance the race that is set before us,*

2. *fixing our eyes on Jesus, the author and perfecter of faith, who for the joy set before Him endured the cross, despising the shame, and has sat down at the right hand of the throne of God.*

3. *For consider Him who has endured such hostility by sinners against Himself, so that you will not grow weary and lose heart.*

My friends, fix your eyes on Jesus. Run the race. Pass the baton.

RESOURCES

Helpful Study Tools

Arthur, Kay
How to Study Your Bible
Eugene, Oregon: Harvest House Publishers

The New Inductive Study Bible
Eugene, Oregon: Harvest House Publishers

Logos Bible Software
Available at www.logos.com.

Greek Word Study Tools

Kittel, G., Friedrich, G., & Bromiley, G.W.
Theological Dictionary of the New Testament, Abridged (also known as Little Kittel)
Grand Rapids, Michigan: W.B. Eerdmans Publishing Company

Zodhiates, Spiros
The Complete Word Study Dictionary: New Testament
Chattanooga, Tennessee: AMG Publishers

Hebrew Word Study Tools

Harris, R.L., Archer, G.L., & Walker, B.K.
Theological Wordbook of the Old Testament (also known as TWOT)
Chicago, Illinois: Moody Press

Zodhiates, Spiros
The Complete Word Study Dictionary: Old Testament
Chattanooga, Tennessee: AMG Publishers

General Word Study Tools

Vine, W.E.
Vine's Complete Expository Dictionary of Old and New Testament Words
Nashville, Tennessee: Thomas Nelson

Strong, James
The New Strong's Exhaustive Concordance of the Bible
Nashville, Tennessee: Thomas Nelson

Recommended Commentary Sets

Expositor's Bible Commentary
Grand Rapids, Michigan: Zondervan

NIV Application Commentary
Grand Rapids, Michigan: Zondervan

The New American Commentary
Nashville, Tennessee: Broadman and Holman Publishers

HOW TO DO AN ONLINE WORD STUDY

For use with www.blueletterbible.org

1. Type in BIble verse. Change the version to NASB. Click the "Search" button.
2. When you arrive at the next screen, you will see six lettered boxes to the left of your verse. Click the "C" button to take you to the concordance link.
3. Click on the Strong's number which is the link to the original word in Greek or Hebrew.

Clicking this number will bring up another screen that will give you a brief definition of the word as well as list every occurrence of the Greek word in the New Testament or Hebrew word in the Old Testmanet. Before running to the dictionary definition, scan places where this word is used in Scripture and examine the general contexts where it is used.

PURCHASE WITH PURPOSE

When you buy books, studies, videos and audios, please purchase from Precept Ministries through our online store (http://store.precept.org/). We realize you may find some of these materials at a lower price through for-profit retailers, but when you buy through us, the proceeds support the work that we do to::

- Develop new Inductive Bible studies
- Translate more studies into other languages
- Support efforts in nearly 185 countries
- Reach millions daily through radio and television
- Train pastors and Bible Study Leaders around the world
- Develop inductive studies for children to start their journey with God
- Equip people of all ages with Bible Study skills that transform lives

*When you buy from Precept, you help to **establish people in God's Word!***

ABOUT PRECEPT

Precept Ministries International was raised up by God for the sole purpose of establishing people in God's Word to produce reverence for Him. It serves as an arm of the church without respect to denomination. God has enabled Precept to reach across denominational lines without compromising the truths of His inerrant Word. We believe every word of the Bible was inspired and given to man as all that is necessary for him to become mature and thoroughly equipped for every good work of life. This ministry does not seek to impose its doctrines on others, but rather to direct people to the Master Himself, who leads and guides by His Spirit into all truth through a systematic study of His Word. The ministry produces a variety of Bible studies and holds conferences and intensive Training Workshops designed to establish attendees in the Word through Inductive Bible Study.

Jack Arthur and his wife, Kay, founded Precept Ministries in 1970. Kay and the ministry staff of writers produce **Precept Upon Precept** studies, **In & Out** studies, **Lord** series studies, the **New Inductive Study Series** studies, **40-Minute studies, and Discover 4 Yourself Inductive Bible Studies for Kids**. From years of diligent study and teaching experience, Kay and the staff have developed these unique, inductive courses that are now used in nearly 185 countries and 70 languages.

MOBILIZING

We are mobilizing believers who "rightly handle the Word of God" and want to use their spiritual gifts and skills to reach 10 million more people with Inductive Bible Study by 2015. If you share our passion for establishing people in God's Word, we invite you to find out more. Visit **www.precept.org/Mobilize** for more detailed information.

ANSWERING THE CALL

Now that you've studied and prayerfully considered the scriptures, is there something new for you to believe or do, or did it move you to make a change in your life? It's one of the many amazing and supernatural results of being in His life-changing Word—God speaks to us.

At Precept Ministries International, we believe that we have heard God speak about our part in the Great Commission. He has told us in His Word to make disciples by teaching people how to study His Word. We plan to reach 10 million more people with Inductive Bible Study by 2015.

If you share our passion for establishing people in God's Word, we invite you to join us! Will you prayerfully consider giving monthly to the ministry? If you give online at **www.precept.org/ATC**, we save on administrative costs so that your dollars go farther. And if you give monthly as an online recurring gift, fewer dollars go into administrative costs and more go toward ministry. Please pray about how the Lord might lead you to answer the call.

INFLUENCE
An Inductive Study on Mentoring

PAM GILLASPIE

Pam Gillaspie, a passionate Bible student and teacher, authors Precept's *Sweeter Than Chocolate!*® and *Cookies on the Lower Shelf*™ Bible study series. Pam holds a BA in Biblical Studies from Wheaton College in Wheaton, Illinois. She and her husband live in suburban Chicago, Illinois with their son, daughter, and Great Dane. Her greatest joy is encouraging others to read God's Word widely and study it deeply . . . precept upon precept.

Connect with Pam at:

www.deepandwide.org

 pamgillaspie

 pamgillaspie

www.ingramcontent.com/pod-product-compliance
Lightning Source LLC
Chambersburg PA
CBHW051352070526
44584CB00025B/3740